国际中文教育武术技术推广系列教材
Wushu Techniques Textbook Series for International Chinese Edu

国际武术联合会
International Wushu Federation
中国武术协会
Chinese Wushu Association
北京体育大学汉语国际推广武术师资培训基地
Wushu Teacher Training Base for Chinese International Promotion of Beijing Sport University

太极拳
Taijiquan

王二平　主编
刘　佳　译

北京体育大学出版社

策划编辑：佟　晖
责任编辑：潘海英
责任校对：赵红霞
版式设计：李　鹤

图书在版编目（CIP）数据

太极拳 : 汉英对照 / 王二平主编 ; 刘佳译. -- 北
京：北京体育大学出版社，2022.6
　　ISBN 978-7-5644-3658-2

　　Ⅰ.①太… Ⅱ.①王… ②刘… Ⅲ.①太极拳 – 汉、
英 Ⅳ.①G852.11

中国版本图书馆CIP数据核字(2022)第089968号

太极拳

TAIJIQUAN

王二平　主编
刘　佳　译

出版发行　北京体育大学出版社
地　　址　北京市海淀区农大南路1号院2号楼2层办公B-212
邮　　编　100084
网　　址　http : //cbs.bsu.edu.cn
发行部　010-62989320
邮购部　北京体育大学出版社读者服务部 010-62989432
印　　刷　唐山玺诚印务有限公司
开　　本　710 mm×1000 mm　　1/16
成品尺寸　170 mm×240 mm
印　　张　14.5
字　　数　256千字
版　　次　2022年6月第1版
印　　次　2022年6月第1次印刷
定　　价　100.00元

国际中文教育武术技术推广系列教材

组织机构

教育部中外语言交流合作中心

北京体育大学

国际武术联合会

中国武术协会

审定委员会

吴　彬　门惠丰　金肖冰

编写委员会

总 主 编：李士英

副总主编：高楚兰　佟　晖

分册主编：王二平　李士英　李英奎

　　　　　林小美　高楚兰

国际中文教育武术技术推广系列教材
《太极拳》编委会

主　编：王二平

副主编：陈伟杰

编　委：孙　瑛　冉千鑫

　　　　杜昊滢　黄雪晴

示　范：黄雪晴

译　者：刘　佳

目录 Contents

武礼篇

Wushu Etiquette

中华武术历史悠久，源远流长，内容丰富多彩、博大精深。源于中国，属于世界的武术运动，深受世界各国人民喜爱，已成为全人类共有的精神、文化财富。

Chinese Wushu (martial arts) goes back to time immemorial, and is well-established, long-standing, and profound. Originating from China, Wushu also belongs to the world, and is greatly admired by people all over the world; it has become a spiritual and cultural asset shared by all.

一、武 礼　　　　Wushu Etiquette

"未曾习武先习礼"，武礼是中国传统的礼法之一。武礼现已成为在国际上一致采用的、具有代表性的、规范统一的武术标准礼法。

武礼的行礼方式包括徒手礼（抱拳礼、注目礼）、持械礼、递械礼和接械礼等。

"Before practicing Wushu, acquire relevant etiquette first." Wushu etiquette is part of China's traditional cultural rule of etiquette, and has become a common practice in the international Wushu community.

Wushu etiquette is represented by barehanded salutes (palm-fist salute; eye salute), weapon-holding salute, weapon-delivering salute, and weapon-receiving salute.

1. 抱拳礼   Palm-fist Salute

抱拳礼的行礼方式是：并步站立，左手四指并拢伸直成掌，拇指屈拢，右手成拳，左掌心掩贴右拳面，左指根线与右拳棱相齐；左掌、右拳胸前相抱，高度与胸平齐，肘尖略下垂，拳、掌与胸间距为20~30厘米；头正，身直，目视受礼者。（图1-1）

抱拳礼的含义是：左掌为文，象征和平，代表武德，寓意孝敬父母、尊敬师长、爱国敬业、诚信友善、仁爱感恩、谦卑简朴；拇指弯曲表示谦虚，寓意武术源于中国，属于世界，应虚心好学、永不自大。右拳为武，象征力量，代表武技，寓意尚武崇德、追求卓越、为国争光、为民服务。左掌盖在右拳上表示爱心、礼让、止戈为武。两手相合，表示习武者要文武兼备、内外兼修，五湖四海天下武林是一家，以武会友、友好团结，弘扬武学文化，造福人类。抱拳礼的寓意为和平、团结和友谊。

The palm-fist salute is as follows: stand with your feet together; the four fingers of your left hand stay straight together as an open palm, with the thumb bent and close to the index finger; the right hand forms a fist, with knuckles pressed against the center of the left palm, and the left palm's finger base line aligned with the right fist's metacarpophalangeal joint line. The fist and palm stay together 20-30 cm away from in front of your chest, with the tips of both elbows slightly drooping. Keep your head and body upright, and gaze at the one receiving the salute. (Fig. 1-1)

The palm-fist salute means: the left palm stands for erudition, symbolizing peace and martial ethics, and implying filial piety to parents, respect for teachers, patriotism, dedication, honesty and friendliness, benevolence and gratitude, humility, and frugality; the bent thumb means modesty, implying that Wushu originates from China and belongs to the world, and that those practicing Wushu should be humble and studious, but never arrogant. The right fist stands for martial arts, symbolizing strength and skills, implying the pursuit of virtue and excellence, glory for the country, and service to the people. The left palm is covered on the right fist to express love, comity, and truce.

The fist meets the palm to indicate that those practicing Wushu must be a master of both the pen and sword, in other words, to be well versed in both polite letters and martial arts. The world's Wushu community is a big family; Wushu is practiced to meet with friends, maintain friendship and unity, and to promote Wushu culture to benefit humanity. In short, the palm-fist salute symbolizes peace, unity, and friendship.

图 1-1　抱拳礼
Fig. 1-1 Palm-fist salute

2. 注目礼　　　　　　　　　　　　　　　　　　　　Eye Salute

注目礼的行礼方法是：并步站立，目视受礼者或向前平视，身体正直，以示对受礼者的恭敬、尊重。若表示答诺或聆听指教受益时，可微点头示意。

The eye salute is as follows: stand with your feet together; gaze at the recipient or look straight ahead; keep your body upright to show respect for the recipient. To respond to an eye salute, you can nod your head slightly.

3. 持械礼   Salute with a Weapon

持械礼是习练武术器械时行的礼节，礼仪内涵同"抱拳礼"。

（1）持剑礼的行礼方法是：并步站立，左手持剑，屈臂，使剑身贴前臂外侧，斜横于胸前；右手拇指屈拢，成斜侧立掌（或剑指），以掌外沿附于左手食指根节，高度与胸平齐，肘微下垂，目视受礼者。（图1-2）

Saluting with a weapon is an etiquette to follow when practicing a weapon, and means the same as the palm-fist salute.

(1) Salute with a sword: stand with your feet together, hold the sword in your left hand, bend your arms, and the blade is attached to the outer edge of the left forearm and diagonally across the chest. Your right palm (or sword finger) stays oblique with the thumb bent, and the palm's outer edge is attached to the joint of the left hand's index finger. This position is at the height where the chest is, with the elbows slightly drooping and eyes on the recipient. (Fig. 1-2)

图 1-2 持剑礼
Fig. 1-2 Sword-holding salute

（2）抱刀礼的行礼方法是：并步站立，左手抱刀，屈臂，使刀横于胸前，刀身斜向下，刀背贴附于前臂之上，刀刃向上；右手拇指屈拢成斜侧立掌，以掌心附在左手拇指第一指节上，高度与胸平齐，肘微下垂，目视受礼者。（图1-3）

(2) Salute with a broadsword: stand with your feet together, hold the broadsword with your left hand, and bend your arms so that the broadsword is horizontal to the chest; the blade is slanted downward, with its spine attached to your forearm, and its belly facing upward. Your right palm stays oblique with the thumb bent, and the palm is attached to the first knuckle of the left thumb. This position is at the height where the chest is, with the elbows slightly drooping and eyes on the recipient. (Fig. 1-3)

图 1-3 抱刀礼
Fig. 1-3 Broadsword-holding salute

（3）持枪礼的行礼方法是：并步站立，右手握枪端，屈臂于胸前，枪身直立，枪尖向上；左手拇指屈拢成侧立掌，掌心与右手指根节指面相贴，高度与胸平齐，肘略下垂，目视受礼者。

(3) Salute with a spear: stand with your feet together, hold the spear in your right hand, with the arms bent in front of the chest; keep the spear upright, with its tip facing upward; keep your left palm in an oblique position with the thumb bent; the palm is in

contact with the right hand's finger joints. This position is at the height where the chest is, with the elbows slightly drooping and eyes on the recipient.

（4）持棍礼的行礼方法是：并步站立，右手握棍把段（靠棍把1/3处），屈臂于胸前，棍身直立，棍梢向上；左手拇指屈拢成侧立掌，掌心与右手指根节指面相贴，高度与胸平齐，肘略下垂，目视受礼者。（图1-4）

(4) Salute with a stick: stand with your feet together, hold the handle of the stick with your right hand (1/3 of the handle), with your arms bent in front of the chest; keep the stick upright, with its tip facing upward; keep your left palm in an oblique position with the thumb bent; the palm is in contact with the right hand's finger joints. This position is at the height where the chest is, with the elbows slightly drooping and eyes on the recipient. (Fig. 1-4)

图 1-4　持棍礼
Fig. 1-4　Stick-holding salute

4. 递械礼   Weapon-delivering Salute

递械礼包括递剑礼、递刀礼、递枪礼和递棍礼等。

（1）递剑礼的行礼方法是：并步站立，左手托护手盘，右手托剑前身，使剑平横于胸前，剑尖向右，目视接剑者。

（2）递刀礼的行礼方法是：并步站立，左手托护手盘，右手托刀前身，使刀平横于胸前，刀刃向里，目视接刀者。

（3）递枪礼的行礼方法是：并步站立，双手靠近握枪于把段处，左手在上，两臂屈圆，使枪垂直于体前，枪尖向上，目视接枪者。

（4）递棍礼的行礼方法是：并步站立，双手靠近握棍于把段（靠棍把1/3处），左手在上，两臂屈圆，使棍垂直竖于体前，棍梢向上，目视接棍者。

其他器械的递械礼参照上述规范统一。

The weapon-delivering salute includes the sword-delivering salute, broadsword-delivering salute, spear-delivering salute, and stick-delivering salute etc.

(1) The sword-delivering salute is as follows: stand with your feet together, hold the cross-guard in your left hand, and support the front section of the blade with your right hand, so that the sword stays horizontal across the chest, with the tip of the sword pointing to the right and eyes on the recipient.

(2) The broadsword-delivering salute is as follows: stand with your feet together, hold the cross-guard in your left hand, and support the front section of the broadsword with your right hand, so that the broadsword stays horizontal across the chest, with the belly of the broadsword facing inward, and eyes on the recipient.

(3) The spear-delivering salute is as follows: stand with your feet together, hold the spear with both hands close to the handle, with your left hand on top and arms rounded; the spear stays vertical in front of your body, with the spear tip facing upward and your eyes on the recipient.

(4) The stick-delivering salute is as follows: stand with your feet together, keep your

hands close and hold the stick by the handle (1/3 of the stick), with your left hand on top and arms rounded, so that the stick stays vertical in front of your body, with the tip of the stick facing upward and your eyes on the recipient.

For the delivering of other weapons, please refer to the above-mentioned methods.

5. 接械礼   Weapon-receiving Salute

接械礼包括接剑礼、接刀礼、接枪礼和接棍礼等。

（1）接剑礼的行礼方法是：开步站立，左手掌心向上，托剑于递剑者两手之间，右手手心向下接握剑柄，目视右手，接剑。

（2）接刀礼的行礼方法是：开步站立，左手掌心向上，托刀于递刀者两手之间，右手手心向下接握刀柄，目视右手，接刀。

（3）接枪礼的行礼方法是：开步站立，两手虎口向上，上下靠拢，左手在上，靠近递枪者手上部接握，目视双手，接枪。

（4）接棍礼的行礼方法是：开步站立，两手虎口向上，上下靠拢，左手在上，靠近递棍者手上部接握，目视双手，接棍。

其他器械的接械礼参照上述规范统一。

The weapon-receiving salute includes the sword-receiving salute, broadsword-receiving salute, spear-receiving salute, and stick-receiving salute etc.

(1) The sword-receiving salute is as follows: stand with your feet apart; your left palm faces upward and supports the sword between the deliverer's hands, and your right palm faces downward and holds the hilt of the sword; eyes on the right hand when receiving the sword.

(2) The broadsword receiving salute is as follows: stand with your feet apart; your left palm faces upward and supports the broadsword between the deliverer's hands, and your right palm faces downward and holds the hilt of the broadsword; eyes on the right hand when receiving the broadsword.

(3) The spear-receiving salute is as follows: stand with your feet apart; the part of the hand between the thumb and the index finger faces upward; hands stay close, with your left hand above your right hand and the deliverer's hands; eyes on both hands when receiving the spear.

(4) The stick-receiving salute is as follows: stand with your feet apart; the part of the hand between the thumb and the index finger faces upward; hands stay close, with your left hand above your right hand and the deliverer's hands; eyes on both hands when receiving the stick.

For the receiving of other weapons, please refer to the above-mentioned methods.

二、武礼的应用　　　　　Applying Wushu Etiquette

队长整队完毕，向老师报告时，师生均行"注目礼"。老师向学生说"上课！"，队长发"敬礼！"口令，学生行"抱拳礼"；老师看学生都行礼端正后，行"抱拳礼"答谢，落手立正；然后学生再落手立正。礼毕，授课开始。

授课结束，队长整队完毕，老师对本节课的整体情况进行总结发言后示意队长发"敬礼！"口令，学生行"抱拳礼"；老师看学生都行礼端正后，行"抱拳礼"答谢，落手立正；然后学生再落手立正。礼毕，老师向学生说"下课！"，老师和学生同时击掌，下课。

After the team leader lines everyone up and reports to the instructor, both the instructor and students salute with their eyes. The instructor says to the students, "Class!", then the team leader gives the "Salute" instruction, and the students perform the palm-fist salute. The instructor will make sure that all students are saluting properly and respond to them with the same position. The instructor then puts down his hands and resumes the position of attention; the students will do the same. After this, the session begins.

At the end of the session, the team leader again lines everyone up, and the instructor recaps on the session and then signals the team leader to give the "Salute" instruction. Then the students perform the palm-fist salute, and the instructor will make sure that all students are saluting properly and respond to them with the same position. The instructor then puts down his hands and resumes the position of attention; the students will do the same. After this, the instructor says, "Class dismissed", and gives students a high five before they leave the class.

2. 专业理论课   Theoretical Sessions

老师走上讲台，向学生说"上课！"，队长发"起立！敬礼！"口令，学生行"抱拳礼"；老师看学生都行礼端正后，行"抱拳礼"答谢，落手立正；然后学生再落手立正，队长发"坐下！"口令。礼毕，学生就座，授课开始。

授课结束，老师向学生说"下课！"，队长发"起立！敬礼！"口令，学生行"抱拳礼"；老师看学生都行礼端正后，行"抱拳礼"答谢，落手立正；然后学生再落手立正，队长发"坐下！"口令。礼毕，学生就座，下课。

The instructor walks up to the podium and says to the students, "Class!", and the team leader follows by shouting out "Stand up! Salute!" The students then perform the palm-fist salute. The instructor will make sure that all students are saluting properly and respond to them with the same position. The instructor then puts down his hands and resumes the position of attention; the students will do the same. The team leader then shouts out "Sit down"! After this, the students are seated, and the session begins.

At the end of the session, the instructor says, "Class dismissed". The team leader shouts out "Stand up! Salute!", then the students perform the palm-fist salute. The instructor will make sure that all students are saluting properly and respond to them with the same position. The instructor then puts down his hands and resumes the position of attention; the students will do the same. The team leader then shouts out "Sit down"! After this, the students are seated, and the session ends.

3. 武术比赛、表演等　　　　　　Wushu Competition and Performance

在武术测试、比赛时，运动员听到点名后应立即进场，面向裁判长，行"抱拳礼"或"持械礼"，待裁判长示意后，即走向起势位置；完成套路后，须并步收势，再转向裁判长行"抱拳礼"或"持械礼"，即可退场；赛后示分时应向裁判长行"抱拳礼"或"持械礼"。

在武术表演时，表演开始前和结束后，表演者应向主席台上的贵宾、前辈和观众行"抱拳礼"或"持械礼"。在武术的社会活动中，表演者受到介绍时应行"抱拳礼"示礼。在交流技术、切磋技艺时，双方也应行"抱拳礼"或"持械礼"。武林同道见面问候、告别时，也应行"抱拳礼"，以体现尊师重道，礼尚往来。

During tests or competitions, athletes should enter the arena immediately upon hearing their names called out, face the referee, and perform the palm-fist salute or weapon-holding salute; after the referee gestures, athletes should go to the starting position, complete the routine, stand at the finishing position, and then turn to the referee to perform the palm-fist salute or weapon-holding salute before leaving the arena. When the scores are announced, athletes should perform the palm-fist salute or weapon-holding salute to the referee.

When performing Wushu, before and after the performance, performers should do the palm-fist salute or weapon-holding salute to the distinguished guests on the rostrum, seniors, and spectators. On social occasions of Wushu, when being introduced, performers should perform the palm-fist salute to show etiquette. When exchanging techniques and discussing skills, both sides should perform the palm-fist salute or weapon-holding salute. When Wushu colleagues greet each other or say goodbye, they should also perform the palm-fist salute to show respect for the instructor and courtesy.

太极拳概述

Overview of Taijiquan

一、认识太极拳　　　　　Cognition of Taijiquan

　　源于中国，属于世界的太极拳运动，历史悠久，源远流长，其内容丰富多彩，博大精深。经过长期的发展，形成了包括各种功法、拳械套路和对抗格斗等注重内外兼修的运动项目。

　　关于太极拳的起源，有许多讲法。但追根溯源，据史料记载，太极拳发源于中国河南省焦作市温县陈家沟，是由陈氏第九世、明末清初人陈王廷在三百多年前创编的。

　　陈王廷，字奏廷（公元1600—1680年）。他以中国古典哲学思想为指导，在祖传拳法和多年研究民间武术的基础上，与儒家、道家学说，导引、吐纳及中医经络学说相结合，融诸家之长为一炉，创编出了动静开合、虚实转换、刚柔相济、快慢相间、老少皆宜的太极拳械套路和推手技法，并依据太极的阴阳对立统一、转化之理来解析拳理，依太极图来规范拳技。

　　"太极"是中国古典哲学中的一个术语，意指派生万物的本原。太极也有多样的文化解释，如本原，阴阳，太初、起始、原点，混沌，大无外、小无内……　"太极"一词最早见于《周易·系辞上》中的"易有太极，是生两仪，两仪生四象，四象生八卦……"。太极是天地万物的根本，是宇宙的原始状态，是天地万物一体的概念，是万物发生的契机与起源，是阴阳二气的开始。太极拳取名此意，即表示含有阴阳动静、虚实变化之意。

　　简言之，太极拳就是以太极之理立论的一种拳术，它不仅要求形神兼备、内外兼修，而且渗透着中国古典哲学、美学、伦理学和医学等深邃丰富的内涵，从而使它具有无尽的东方文化魅力。太极拳的文化渊源是中国传统文化，太极拳的本质属性是武术技击性和养生性，太极拳的运动形式是功法修炼、套路演练和对抗格斗，太极拳是注重内外兼修的民族性体育项目。

太极拳是一种柔和、缓慢、轻灵、沉稳、刚柔相济，注重本体感觉、自我控制和意气引导的拳术。太极拳的拳术特点有中正安舒、不偏不倚、心静体松、呼吸自然、轻灵沉着、圆活连贯、上下相随，连绵不断、虚实分明、柔中寓刚、以意导动、意动势随、势正劲整等。太极拳的动作特点有中止圆活、行云流水、动静有序、快慢相间、刚柔相济、平和自然等。

Taijiquan, which originated in China and belongs to the world, has a long history and is well-established and profound; After a long-term development, it has become a type of sports that pay attention to both internal and external training, including various skills, boxing and weapon routines and confrontation fighting.

There are many legends about the origin of Taijiquan, but according to historical records, Taijiquan originated in Chenjiagou, Wen County, Jiaozuo City, Henan Province, China; it was created more than 300 years ago by Chen Wangting, the ninth of the Chen family, from the late Ming Dynasty to the early Qing Dynasty.

Chen Wangting, also called Zouting (1600-1680 AD), drew on Chinese classical philosophy, ancestral boxing and many years of research on folk Wushu. He absorbed ideas from Confucianism, Taoism, Daoyin, Tuna, and TCM meridian theories, combining the advantages of all schools into one. Taijiquan integrates the combination of dynamic and static opening and closing, virtual and actual transformation, rigidity and softness, speed and slowness, and is suitable for all ages. Taijiquan develops weapon routines and hand pushing techniques, reflects the theory of boxing based on the principle of the unity and transformation of yin and yang in Taiji, and regulate boxing skills based on the Taiji diagram.

"Taiji" is a term in Chinese classical philosophy, which means the origin of all things. Taiji also has various cultural explanations, such as origin, Yin and Yang, Taichu, chaos, big without outside and small without inside... The word "Taiji" was first discovered in *Zhou Yi*, recording "Yi has Taiji, which produces Liangyi, Liangyi produces Sixiang, and Sixiang produces Bagua...". Taiji is the foundation of all things in heaven and earth, the original state of the universe, the concept of the integration of all things in the universe, the opportunity and origin of all, and the beginning of Yin and Yang. Taijiquan is named after it, which means that it contains the movement of Yin and Yang and the change of deficiency and reality.

In short, Taijiquan is a kind of boxing based on the theory of Taiji. It not only requires both form and spirit, inside and outside, but also permeates the profound and rich connotation of Chinese classical philosophy, aesthetics, ethics and medicine, so that it demonstrates endless Oriental cultural charm. Taijiquan originates in Chinese traditional culture. The essential attribute of Taijiquan includes Wushu skills and health-enhancing philosophy. Taijiquan includes skill cultivation, routine exercise and confrontation fighting. Taijiquan is a national sports project that pays attention to both internal and external cultivation.

Taijiquan is a kind of boxing that is mild, slow, light, calm, vigorous and soft, enhancing noumenon feeling, self-control and spirit guidance. Taijiquan features peace and comfort, impartiality, calmness and relaxation, natural breathing, lightness, flexibility and coherence, coordination, contuinuity, clear deficiency and reality, vigor in softness, guidance by intention, etc. The practice of Taijiquan should be flexible, smooth, quiet, rapid and slow, vigorous and soft, peaceful and natural.

1. 太极拳的文化渊源是中国传统文化　The Origin of Taijiquan in Chinese Traditional Culture

太极拳是古代先贤，以中国传统文化《易经》的思想，黄老学说（黄老学说指的是《黄帝内经》以及老子的《道德经》所表达的思想）以及兵家思想等作为基础创造出来的拳道。太极拳是中华武术里哲理极深、意境极高的拳术。练拳者如果没有深厚的传统文化底蕴，是很难真正体悟太极拳的博大精深、意境高远的思想的。太极拳在发展过程中，深受中国传统文化的影响，自然地融汇了易学、哲学、中医、伦理、宗教、军事、文艺、美学、养生等多种文化思想和文化观念，并以此为理论和技术的依据，逐渐形成了有着深刻思想内涵、独具民族特色的太极武学。其内涵丰富、寓意深邃，既具备了人类体育运动强身健体的共同特性，又有中华民族所特有的哲理性、科学性和艺术性。太极拳是中国传统文化的具体表现和中国人民智慧的结晶。

Taijiquan is a kind of boxing created by ancient sages based on the thought of *The Book of Changes*, Huang Lao theory (Huang Lao theory refers to the thought expressed in the *Yellow Emperor's Internal Classic* and Lao Tzu's *Tao Te Ching*) and strategist thought. Taijiquan is a boxing with profound philosophy and high artistic conception in Chinese Wushu. Without profound traditional culture, it is difficult for practitioners to truly understand the broad and profound thought of Taijiquan. In the process of its development, Taijiquan has been deeply influenced by Chinese traditional culture. It naturally integrates various cultural thoughts and cultural concepts such as Yi ology, philosophy, traditional Chinese medicine, ethics, religion, military science, literature, art, aesthetics and health-enhancing philosophy. In this sense, Taijiquan has gradually formed a Taiji Wushu with profound ideological connotation and unique national characteristics. Its connotation is rich and profound. It not only has the common characteristics of sports to strengthen the body, but also possesses the unique philosophy, science and art of the Chinese nation. Taijiquan is the concrete expression of Chinese traditional culture and the crystallization of the wisdom of Chinese people.

2. 太极拳的本质属性是武术技击性和养生性　　The Essential Attribute of Taijiquan including Wushu Skills for Attacking and Health-enhancing Philosophy

　　武术技击性技术范畴包括用于实战技击的功法，徒手的踢、打、摔、拿、跳跃等，器械的劈、砍、扎、击等攻防格斗法。太极拳械套路就是以这些基本技击动作和养生动作为主要内容编排形成的。其养生性主要包括太极拳本身的健身作用和以导引、吐纳、保健、养身、养心、养气等为内容的功法套路等。太极拳与气功相通。太极拳虽然是武术的拳种之一，但其养生功能和发挥的作用又有别于武术的其他项目，所以太极拳也是人类的保健养生运动。体育无国界，太极拳已成为世界性的体育项目。

The technical category of Wushu skills includes the techniques used in actual combat skills, unarmed kicking, beating, wrestling, holding, jumping, etc., and offensive and defensive combat methods such as cutting, slashing, piercing, and striking with weapons. Taiji weapon repertoire is based on the main content of these basic Wushu movements and vitality. Its health-enhancing philosophy mainly includes the fitness function of Taijiquan and the exercise routines, such as skills of inner guiding, breathing, health care, physical and mental cultivation, Qi nourishment and so on. Taiji is connected with Qigong. Although Taiji is one of the types of Wushu, its health-enhancing function and role are different from other Wushu skills. Therefore, Taiji is also a type of healthy exercise for human beings. There are no national borders in the field of sports, and Taiji has become a worldwide sport.

3. 太极拳的运动形式是功法修炼、套路演练和对抗格斗
The Exercising Forms of Taijiquan including Skill Cultivation, Routine Exercise and Confrontation Fighting

　　太极拳的功法修炼动作易学易练，套路演练使太极拳攻防、养生技术具有一定艺术性，包括传统各式太极拳械和国际标准的各式太极拳械、对练等。对抗格斗是太极拳攻防技术在双方直接对抗中的应用，包括太极推手、太极散手技击法等。太极拳的功法、套路和格斗三者有着密切的内在联系。太极拳的运动形式属于体育范畴，但又区别于其他体育项目。

　　Taijiquan is easy to learn and exercise. Routine exercises make Taijiquan artistic in the attack and defense and health preservation. It includes all kinds of traditional Taijiquan weapons, international standard Taijiquan weapons, pair exercises, etc. Confrontation fighting is the application of attack-and-defense technology in the direct confrontation between the two sides, including Taiji hand-pushing, Taijishou and so on. There is a close internal relationship among the skills, routines and fighting in Taijiquan. Taijiquan is a distinguished type of sport.

4. 太极拳是注重内外兼修的民族性体育运动项目
Taijiquan as a National Sport Emphasizing both Internal and External Cultivation

太极拳是中国人民在长期劳动实践中，不断总结创造的具有民族特色的一项体育运动项目。太极拳提倡内练精、气、神，外练筋、骨、皮，内修德、外修武，内外合一，松静自然，天人合一。太极拳不仅是一种功法技艺精湛的拳种，而且是一种中华民族优秀的传统文化，与文、史、哲、理、医等诸多学科有着血肉难分的联系和相互渗透的渊源，归属于人体生命科学的范畴。太极拳的文化渊源是中国传统文化，其运动的方式方法体现了浓重的民族意识和民族性，是独有的中国特色。太极拳是中国传统文化中一颗璀璨的明珠，是中华民族对世界文明的贡献。

Taijiquan is a sport with national characteristics that Chinese people have constantly summarized and created in their long-term labor practice. Taijiquan advocates internal practice of vigor, Qi and spirit, external practice of tendons, bones and skin, internal cultivation of morality and external cultivation of Wushu, internal and external integration, relaxation, tranquility and the integration of heaven and man. Taijiquan is not only a kind of boxing with exquisite skills, but also an excellent traditional culture in China. It has inseparable relationship and mutual penetration with many disciplines such as literature, history, philosophy, science and medicine, and belongs to the category of human life science. Taijiquan originates in Chinese traditional culture. Its way of movement reflects a strong national consciousness and nationality, which is a unique Chinese characteristic. Taijiquan is a shining pearl in Chinese traditional culture. It is Chinese contribution to the world civilization.

二、太极拳的内容　　　　　　　　　　Content of Taijiquan

太极拳的内容丰富多彩，按其运动形式可分为功法运动、套路运动和格斗运动。

Taijiquan is profound. According to its movement form, it can be divided into skill movement, routine movement and fighting movement.

1. 太极拳的功法运动　　　　　　　Taijiquan Skill Movement

太极拳功法是为了掌握太极拳套路，健身养生，提高对抗格斗技术，发掘人体潜能，围绕发展体能、技能和心理品质的专门修炼方式。太极拳功法具有健身、养生、修身、养性及增强技击能力等作用。它包括有提高肢体关节活动幅度和肌肉伸缩性能的柔功，锻炼意、气、劲、形完整一体的内功，增强肢体攻击力度和抗击能力的外壮功，以养生、修心、悟道为主的太极养生功，锻炼入静、放松及培根固本的桩功，练习步法的行功及臂功、腰功、裆功、腿功、眼功、耳功等多种功法。太极拳功法，动作简单，易学易练，简便易行，可以独自练习，也可集体练习；它内外兼练，性命双修，动静结合，壮内强外，形式多样，而且锻炼部位全面，整体性较强。"练拳不练功，到老一场空"，从套路、格斗、健身、养生、修心、防身等诸方面讲，练习太极拳功法都是非常重要的。练功使精足，则精力充沛、不畏寒暑；气足，则声音洪亮、百病不侵；神足，则两目炯炯、益寿延年。太极拳功法就是精、气、神修炼法。此外，套路的练习如没有进行基本功的功法练习，也只能是学得皮毛，形神全无，格斗的话也只能是有招无功总还是空。练习太极拳功法，将会使练拳者受益无穷。太极拳功法随太极拳运动的萌生而产生，随太极拳运动的发展而发展，并随太极拳的技术演进而变化。

Taijiquan exercises are designed to master Taijiquan routines, keep fit, improve fighting skills, induce the human potential for Wushu, and focus on the development of physical stamina, skills, and psychological qualities. Taijiquan exercises have the functions of enhancing fitness, health preservation, self-cultivation, nourishment and development of Wushu ability. It includes soft power that improves the range of motion of the limbs and joints and muscle contraction, the internal power exercises that integrates mind, Qi, strength and shape, and the external strength exercises that enhance the body's attack strength and resistance. It focuses on health preservation, mind cultivation, and enlightenment. Taiji health skills include Zhuang Gong for calmness, relaxation and solid foundation, as well as Xing Gong for arms, waist, stance, leg, eyes, ears, etc. Taijiquan includes simple movements, easy to learn and practice, and can be practiced alone or in groups; it can be practiced both internally and externally, both physically and mentally; it combines movement and quietness, and enhances both internal and external health in various forms. Taijiquan is a kind of comprehensive exercises that has strong unity. " One who pratices boxing without practice in basic training will eventually faill." From the aspects of routine, fighting, fitness, health, mind training, self-defense, etc., the practice of Taijiquan is very important. Exercises will make you energetic and not afraid of cold and heat; Qi will make your voice loud and body invincible; high spirit will bring you piercing eyes and prolong life. Taijiquan exercises focus on the cultivation methods of Jing, Qi, and spirit. In addition, if the routine practice does not include the basic skills, it can only be learned incompletely without the mastery of its spirit. In the case of fighting, it can only be a trick. Taiji exercises will benefit the learners infinitely. Taijiquan exercises came into being with the birth of Taijiquan and changed with the technological evolution.

2. 太极拳的套路运动　　　　　　　　Routine Exercise of Taijiquan

太极拳套路由风格各异的技术动作组成，蕴含哲理，具有攻防内涵和很高的观赏价值，给人以美的享受。人们按照不同的需要和目的，创编成不同结构、不同特点、不同运动强度，具有技击性、健身性、艺术性的太极拳套路。套路运动是以技击动作和养生动作为素材，按攻守进退、刚柔相济的运动变化规律编成的整套练习形式。套路运动按练习形式可分为单练、对练和集体演练。

Taijiquan routine exercise consists of technical movements with different styles. It contains philosophy, attack-and-defense connotation and high admiration value, which gives people the artistic enjoyment. According to different needs and purposes, people create Taijiquan routines possessing different structures, different characteristics and exercise intensity as well as attacking and artistic characteristics. Routine movement is a complete set of practice form based on the movement of combat and health-enhancement. It features in offense and defense, stepping forward and backward and the combination of vigor and suppleness. Routine movment can be divided into single practice, pair practice and group practice according to the form of practice.

3. 太极拳的格斗运动　　　　　　　　　Fighting Movement of Taijiquan

太极拳格斗运动是两人或两人以上在一定条件下，按照一定的规则进行斗智斗勇、较技较力的对抗性练习形式。

（1）太极推手：太极推手是两人按照一定的规则，使用掤、捋、挤、按、采、挒、肘、靠等技法，按沾、连、粘、随的原则，通过肌肉的感觉来判断对方的用劲，然后引进落空，借力打力，将对方推出，以此来切磋技艺的练习和竞赛项目。其主要是太极拳练习过程中的一种锻炼手段。

（2）太极散手：太极散手是将传统技击术和现代技击术相结合，运用快速的踢、打、摔、拿、掤、捋、挤、按、采、挒、肘、靠等综合技击方法制胜对方，使格斗达到最简单、最直接、最实用、最有效的运动方式。太极散手技术基本归类为实战姿势即太极式、步法、防守法、跌法、踢法、打法、摔法、擒拿法和防守反击法，以及太极八法、战术运用等。

Taijiquan fighting is a form of confrontational practice in which two or more people fight against each other with wits, courage, skills and power according to certain rules in certain conditions.

(1) Taiji hand-pushing: Taiji hand-pushing is an exercise and competition in which two people use the techniques of "warding-off, rolling-back, pressing, pushing, pushing-down, picking, splitting, elbowing, leaning, etc." according to certain rules to judge each other's strength through the feeling of muscles according to the principles of touching, connecting, sticking and following, and then introduce failure, use strength to push each other out, so as to compare skills. It is mainly a means of exercise in the process of Taijiquan practice.

(2) Taiji Sanshou(bare-handed fighting): Taiji Sanshou combines traditional and modern attacking techniques, and adopts comprehensive attacking skills such as fast kick, hit, wrestling, holding, warding-off, rolling-back, pressing, pushing-down, picking, splitting, elbowing, leaning, etc. to win the opponent, so as to make fighting the simplest, direct, most practical and effective way of movement. Taiji Sanshou techniques are basically classified into actual combat postures, namely Taiji style, techniques of step, defense, dropping,kicking, hitting, wrestling, catching and holding, defensive counter attack, as well as the Eight Techniques of Taiji, tactical application, etc.

三、太极拳的作用   Role of Taijiquan

太极拳不仅仅是一种身体运动，还是一种生活方式、一种教育手段、一种精神载体，是培养健康体魄、塑造健全人格、促进人的全面发展的有效途径。为使太极拳更好地服务于世界人民，为人类的健康造福，国家应开展全方位、丰富多彩的国际太极拳交流活动，不断挖掘和充分展现太极拳运动的综合社会价值和作用，增进各国人民的人文交流与文明互鉴，为中华武术生生不息、永续发展，推动共建人类命运共同体，促进世界和平发展作出独特而积极的贡献。

Taijiquan is not only a type of physical exercise, but also a way of life, an educational means and a spiritual carrier. It is an effective way to cultivate healthy physique, shape sound personality and promote people's all-round development. In order to make Taijiquan better serve the people of the world and benefit human health, the state has carried out all-round and colorful international Taijiquan exchange activities, constantly excavating and fully displaying the comprehensive social value and role of Taijiquan, enhancing people-to-people and cultural exchanges and mutual learning among all the countries, and contributing to the continuous and sustainable development of Chinese Wushu, promoting the construction of a community with a shared future for mankind and making unique and positive contributions to world peace and development.

1. 养生 Health Enhancement

太极养生是以平衡、和谐、自然的太极核心理念为指导，为预防疾病、保持健康、保养生命而采取的太极拳修炼为主体，配以养身、养心、养气等活动和多种保健措施，达到增强体质、延年益寿目的的养生之道，其涵盖我们的衣、食、住、行等生活的方方面面，通过各种方法颐养生命。人应顺应自然环境、四时气候的变化，主动调整自我，保持与大自然的和谐统一，每个人都应构建适合自己的个体太极养生模式。人们应遵循动静有序、饮食有节、起居有常、劳逸有度、平和静心、爱心感恩、谦卑简朴、形神共养、内外兼修、道法自然、天地人合的原则。太极拳养生功效明显，练习太极拳，可以使每个人都成为"上工治未病"的高明医生。

Taiji health enhancement is guided by the core concept of balance, harmony and nature. It takes Taiji cultivation as the main body to prevent diseases, maintain health and life, coupled with activities such as physical and mental cultibation and Qi nourishment and a variety of health care measures, so as to achieve the purpose of strengthening physique and prolonging life. It covers all aspects of our life, such as clothing, food, housing and transportation, and takes care of our lives through various methods. People should adapt to the changes of natural environment and four seasons' climate, actively adjust themselves and maintain harmony and unity with nature. Everyone should build an individual Taiji health enhancement model suitable for himself. People should follow the principles of orderly movement and quietness, regular diet and daily life, moderate work and leisure, peace and meditation, love and gratitude, humility and simplicity, joint cultivation of form and spirit, internal and external cultivation, Taoism and nature, and the harmony among heaven, earth and man. Taijiquan can achieve the effect of health enhancement. Practicing Taijiquan can make everyone a wise doctor who "goes to work to cure disease".

2.防身 Self Defense

太极拳是快慢相间、刚柔相济的拳术，以武术的技击动作为主要内容。太极拳的实质是慢练快用。太极拳慢练是为了放松，平心静气，去除身上的僵劲和拙力，去紧求松；快用则是出手、出腿的速度要快，运用腰胯整劲。只有在太极拳慢练放松的基础上，速度才能更快。太极拳技击法是体现武术攻防本质的属性，将传统技击术与现代技击术相结合，利用一切可利用的手段，以最大力量攻击其弱点，使其失去平衡，并保持自身平衡。太极拳技击要求招无定法，一招多用，想哪打哪，意到拳到，随机应变；有形归无迹，无过不及，自然而然，有无间一片神行；上封眼下踢裆，中间穿心肘，擒拿手指弱胜强；周身无处不是拳，挨到何处何处击。

Taijiquan is a type of boxing with the combination of rapidness and slowness, vigor and suppleness. Its main content is the attack of Wushu. The essence of Taijiquan is to practice systematically and apply quickly. The systematic training of Taijiquan is to relax, calm down and remove stiff and awkward force of the body; it also intends to exchange tightness to suppleness. Quick application means that the movement of hand and leg should be fast, and the strength of waist and crotch should be used. Only on the basis of slow practice and relaxation can the speed be faster. Taijiquan technique is an attribute that reflects the essence of attack and defense of Wushu. It combines traditional techniques with modern attacking techniques, and adopts all available means to attack the opponent's weaknesses with maximum strength, make him out of balance, and maintain your own balance. There are no fixed rules for the movements which can be used in many ways. One is free to hit wherever he wants with the fist striking as soon as Yi(the mind) appears. There is spirit in materials. Follow the rules of nature and be in harmony with the universe. Cover your eyes, kick the crotch, hit the middle with elbow and conquer strength with weakness by catch-and-hold finger control. Every part of the body can be used as a fist and it hits wherever it goes.

3. 修心   Mental Cultivation

　　太极拳修心是静心修炼太极武学的平衡之术，爱心修炼太极养生的和谐之法，恒心修炼太极心经的自然之道。修炼太极拳，需要"平衡、和谐、自然"，六字箴言，大道至简，贵在坚持，修心为先。太极拳理可应用于日常生活和工作之中，体现在为人之道"中正安舒，不偏不倚"，处世之道"轻灵圆活，刚柔相济"，立身之道"无过不及，自然而然"，成功之道"连绵不断，快慢相间"。练习太极拳只有以中正为核心，才能辐射四方；不执迷，能放得下，方可达到轻灵；能看到"己"，还要看到"他"，如此才能刚柔相济。有得有失，进退之间，云淡风轻，自然是人的天性，符合了天性，才能和谐自如。无得失心，有进取意，这是太极拳的成功学韬略。练拳者如能体会并做到这几方面，就实现人拳合一了。太极拳的精华蕴涵在形之中，却又在形之外，它在人们的内心。太极拳的重点是养心修心，去繁从简，道法自然，清静无为。通过修心和拳法运动来领悟太极精髓。付出爱心善行不求回报，遇到挫折逆境心存感激，谦卑简朴平和自然生活，有衣有食有栖身之处应知足常乐，静中生慧，享受心灵富足。太极有道，道生自然，生生不息，爱心永恒。太极生活化，生活太极化，体验感悟平衡、和谐、自然的太极人生，找到一本属于自己的太极心经。

Mental cultivation in Taijiquan focuses on the balance skill of meditation and cultivation of Taiji Wushu and the harmonious philosophy of Taiji health enhancement with benevolence and the natural law of Taiji Heart Sutra. Practicing Taijiquan requires "balance, harmony and nature". Less is more. The six-character proverb needs persistent practice where the mental cultivation takes the priority. Taijiquan theory can be applied to daily life and work, which is reflected in the way of being "upright, comfortable and impartial", the way of dealing with relationship (being gentle, agile, flexible and active with vigor and suppleness), the way of conducting oneself (no excess, following the nature law) and the way of success ("continuous, alternating between rapidness and slowness"). Only by taking Zhongzheng as the core, can Taijiquan be promoted widely; If you are not obsessive and just let it go, you can achieve gentleness and flexibility; if you can see both "yourself" and "the other", you can achieve a balance between vigor and suppleness; if you can balance gain and loss, you can keep calm and harmonious and be in line with nature. This is the successful strategy of Taijiquan. If practitioners can understand and achieve these aspects, they will realize the harmony between man and fist. The essence of Taijiquan lies in form, both inside and outside. It is in the inner heart of people. The focus of Taijiquan is to cultivate the mind, get rid of complexity and keep simplify, and pursue "Taoism follwing nature" and "being quiet". Try to understand the essence of Taiji through mental cultivation and boxing. Provide love; do good deeds without asking for return; be grateful in case of setbacks and adversity; be humble, simple and peaceful; live a natural life; be satisfied with clothes, food and shelter. The practitioner enjoys the abundance of spirit and obtains wisdom through peace and quietness. Taiji has Tao. Tao is born naturally and endlessly. Love is eternal. Make Taiji as part of your life, experience and understand the balance, harmony and nature in Taiji, and find a Taiji Heart Sutra of your own.

太极拳基本动作

Basic Movements of Taijiquan

一、手 型   Hand Forms

太极拳的手型要求自然舒展，不可僵硬，不可用拙力僵劲，练习中要松紧互用、虚实互变、无过不及。

主要有拳、掌、勾三种基本手型，规格要领如下：

The hand form of Taijiquan requires natural stretching, no stiffness, and no clumsy strength. In practice, it is necessary to combine relaxation and tightness, change between Xu and Shi (emptiness and solidness) without excess and deficiency.

There are three basic hand forms: fist, palm and hook. The key points are as follows:

1. 拳   Fist

五指卷屈，拇指压于食指、中指第二指节上，自然握拳，不可太紧或太松，拳面要平。（图3-1）

Fold fingers into a fist with the thumb over and press the thumb on the second knuckle of the index finger and middle finger. Naturally clench your fist, not too tight or too loose, and the fist face should be flat. (Fig. 3-1)

图 3-1 拳
Fig. 3-1 Fist

2.掌 Palm

　　五指自然舒展，掌心微含，虎口呈弧形，手指不可僵直，也不可松软弯曲。（图3-2）

　　The five fingers are stretched naturally; the center of the palm shapes a circle and maintains it; the part of the hand between the thumb and the index finger is curved. The fingers should not be stiff or bent softly. (Fig. 3-2)

图 3-2　掌
Fig. 3-2 Palm

3.勾 Hooking

　　五指第一指节自然捏拢，屈腕，五指聚拢，指尖自然向下，不可过于用力下勾，也不可指尖上翘。（图3-3）

　　Naturally squeeze the first knuckles of the five fingers together, bend the wrists, and bunch the five fingers with the fingertips naturally facing down. (Fig. 3-3)

图 3-3　勾
Fig. 3-3 Hooking

二、步 型　　　　　　　　　　　　　　　Step Forms

　　太极拳的各种步型要求自然稳健、虚实分明、屈膝松胯、敛臀提肛、头领气沉，保证步型能运转自如。

Various steps of Taijiquan are required to be natural and steady, have a clear distinction between emptiness and solidness, bend the knees and relax the crotch, tighten the hips and lift the anus, and pull up the head with Qi gathering down to ensure that the steps can operate freely.

1. 弓步　　　　　　　　　　　　　　　　　　Bowing Step

　　两脚全脚掌着地，屈膝前弓，左腿膝关节垂直于脚背，不超出脚尖；右腿自然伸直，脚尖内扣，两脚横向间距10～30厘米，右脚脚跟踏实，勿掀脚拔跟。（图3-4）

Touch the the ground with the whole soles of two feet, bend the knees forward and form an arch, and the knee joint of the left leg is perpendicular to the back of the instep and does not extend beyond the toes; the right leg is naturally straightened with the toes pointing inward. The horizontal distance between the two feet is 10-30 cm, and the right heel should be firm. Do not lift the heel. (Fig. 3-4)

图 3-4　弓步
Fig. 3-4 Bowing step

2. 仆步 — Crouching Step

一腿屈膝全蹲，膝关节与脚尖稍外撇；另一腿自然伸直，平铺接近地面，脚尖内扣；两脚全脚掌着地。（图3-5）

Bend the knee on one leg and squat with knee joints and toes slightly turning outward; the other leg is naturally straightened and laid flat close to the ground, with the toes pointing inward; both feet are on the ground. (Fig. 3-5)

图 3-5　仆步
Fig. 3-5 Crouching step

3. 虚步 — Empty Step

一腿屈膝半蹲，全脚掌着地，脚尖斜向前；另一腿微屈，前脚掌或脚跟着地。（图3-6）

Bend one leg and crouch, and the whole sole of the foot is on the ground, with the toes diagonally pointing forward; the other leg is slightly bent, and the forefoot or heel is on the ground. (Fig. 3-6)

图 3-6　虚步
Fig. 3-6 Empty step

4. 独立步   Single-leg Step

一腿自然直立，另一腿屈膝提起，大腿高于水平位，小腿及脚尖自然下垂，上体保持中正，头领气沉。（图3-7）

One leg is naturally upright; the other leg is bent and lifted; the position of the thigh is higher than the horizontal level; the lower leg and toes are naturally drooping; the upper body remains upright, and the head is pulled up with Qi gathering down. (Fig. 3-7)

图 3-7 独立步
Fig. 3-7 Single-leg step

5. 平行步   Parallel-feet Step

两脚分开，脚尖向前，屈膝下蹲或自然直立，两脚外缘同肩宽。（图3-8）

Separate your feet with toes facing forward, bend your knees and squat or stand upright naturally with the outer edges of your feet maintaining the same width as your shoulders. (Fig. 3-8)

图 3-8 平行步
Fig. 3-8 Parallel-feet step

三、身 型　　　　　　　　　　　　　　　Body Forms

太极拳的身型要求松胯敛臀，含胸拔背，沉肩坠肘，虚领顶劲；上悬下沉，中节舒松；中正安舒，不偏不倚，无过不及；口闭齿扣，舌抵上腭；精神集中，心平气和，气沉丹田；体松心静，呼吸自然。（图3-9）

（1）头：虚领顶劲，下颌微内收，不可偏歪摇摆。

（2）颈：自然竖直，肌肉不可紧张，不可前伸后勾。

（3）肩：保持松沉，不可上耸，也不可后张或前扣。

（4）肘：沉坠松垂，自然弯曲，不可僵直或扬起外翻。

（5）胸：自然舒松，微含，不可外挺或内缩。

（6）背：舒展拔伸，自然放松，不可弓背。

（7）腰：松活自然，不可后弓或前挺。

（8）脊：中正竖直，不可左右歪扭倾斜。

（9）臀：下垂收敛，不可后突或摇摆。

（10）胯：松胯正身，不可僵挺或内收凸臀，不可左右凸出歪扭。

（11）膝：屈伸松活，柔和自然，膝关节与脚尖同向。

The body forms of Taijiquan include relaxing the crotch and tightening the hip, relaxing the chest and drawing the back, sinking the shoulders and dropping the elbows, and erecting the head and relaxing the neck naturally; inpractice, one should pull up the head, gather Qi and relax the middle part of the body; achieve Zhong and Zheng (harmony and perfection) and calmness with no deficiency or excess; the mouth is closed and the tongue is against the upper palate; be concentrated and calm, and gather Qi into Dantian (lower abdomen); relax the body, calm down and breathe naturally. (Fig. 3-9)

(1) Head: erect the head and relax the neck naturally; do not stick out the lower jaw.

(2) Neck: keep it upright naturally; the muscles should not be tense, and it should

not be stretched forward or backward.

(3) Shoulder: keep them relaxed and dropped; do not shrug up, nor stretch back or buckle forward.

(4) Elbow: keep them relaxed, dropped and naturally bent. They should not be stiff or raised everted.

(5) Chest: keep it relaxed and in natural posture, not outward or inward.

(6) Back: stretch and relax it naturally. Don't bow your back.

(7) Waist: keep it relaxed, flexible and natural. Do not bow back or straighten forward.

(8) Ridge: keep it upright and erect. Do not skew or tilt left and right.

(9) Buttocks: drop and tighten buttocks. Do not make backward protrusion or swing.

(10) Crotch: relax the crotch and keep the body upright. Do not make it stiff or retract the convex buttocks, nor protrude or twist left and right.

(11) Knee: bend and extend them freely, keep them soft and natural, and the knee joints are in the same direction as the toes.

图 3-9　太极拳身型
Fig. 3-9 Body Forms

太极拳动作技法

Movement Techniques
of Taijiquan

一、手　法　　　　　　　　　　　　　Hand Techniques

（一）拳掌法 Fist and Palm Techniques

（1）冲拳：拳自腰间旋转向前冲打，由拳心向上逐渐转为拳眼向上，力达拳面。（图4-1）

(1) Punching fist: The fist rotates forward from the waist and punches, gradually turning from the heart of the fist upward to the eye of the fist upward, with the force reaching the face of fist. (Fig. 4-1)

图 4-1　冲拳
Fig. 4-1 Punching fist

（2）冲拳（掩手肱捶）：拳经胸前内旋向前冲打，拳心向下，力达拳面。（图4-2）

(2) Punching fist (covering hands and striking with fist): The fist rushes forward through the front of the chest and rotates forward, with the heart of the fist facing down and force reaching the face of fist. (Fig. 4-2)

图4-2　冲拳（掩手肱捶）
Fig. 4-2　Punching fist (Covering hands and striking with fist)

2. 贯拳   Penetrating Fist

两拳自下经两侧，向前上方弧形圈打，拳眼斜向下，腕与耳平，两臂呈弧形。（图4-3）

The two fists pass through both sides from the bottom, and strike in an arc circle from the front to the top; the fist eyes are inclined downward; the wrists maintain a horizontal level with the ears, and the two arms are arc-shaped. (Fig. 4-3)

图4-3　贯拳
Fig. 4-3　Penetrating fist

3. 推掌   Pushing Palm

臂由屈而伸，掌经耳旁肩上，向前推出，腕与肩平，力达掌根。（图 4-4）

The arms are flexed and stretched; the palms pass through the shoulders next to the ears, and push forward. The wrists maintain a horizontal level with the shoulders, and the force reaches the base of the palms. (Fig. 4-4)

图 4-4 推掌
Fig. 4-4 Pushing palm

（二）臂法 Arm Techniques

1. 掤   Bing (Warding off)

屈臂呈弧形举于体前，掌心向内，力达前臂上外侧。（图4-5）

The flexed arm is held in an arc in front of the body with palms facing inward, and the force reaches the upper and outer side of the forearm. (Fig. 4-5)

图 4-5 掤
Fig. 4-5 Bing (Warding off)

2. 捋   Lü (Rolling back)

臂呈弧形，单手或双手向左或右、侧后捋带，臂须外旋成内旋，动作走弧形。（图4-6）

The arm is in an arc shape. One hand or both hands stroke the belt to the left, right and side. The arm must rotate from outside to inside and move in an arc. (Fig. 4-6)

图 4-6 捋
Fig. 4-6 Lü (Rolling back)

3. 挤   Ji (Pressing)

一臂屈于胸前，另一手搭扶于屈臂手的腕部或前臂内侧，两臂同时前挤，撑圆。（图4-7）

Bend one arm in front of the chest, and put the other hand on the wrist or inside of the forearm of the bent arm. Two arms press forward simultaneously and form a circle. (Fig. 4-7)

图 4-7 挤
Fig. 4-7 Ji (Pressing)

4. 按 An (Pushing)

单掌或双掌自上而下为下按，自后经下向前弧形按推。（图4-8）

A single palm or double palms push downwards from top to bottom, and push forward arcuately from back to bottom. (Fig. 4-8)

图 4-8　按
Fig. 4-8　An (Pushing)

5. 采 Cai (Pulling down)

用手掌按着对方的手臂，由上而下、由下而上或由外向里、由里向外推按沉托采拿。（图4-9）

Press the opponent's arm with the palm of your hand; push it from top to bottom, from bottom to top or from outside to inside, and from inside to outside. (Fig. 4-9)

图 4-9　采
Fig. 4-9　Cai (Pulling down)

6. 捌 — Lie (Splitting)

向外横推或向侧后采带的劲，使对方身体前俯后仰扭转而失重。（图4-10）

The movement of pushing outwards horizontally or pulling the belt back to the side causes the opponent's body to bend forward and backward and lose the center of weight. (Fig. 4-10)

图 4-10　捌
Fig. 4-10　Lie (Splitting)

7. 肘 — Zhou (Elbowing)

以肘部粘着对方肢体向外顶推或以肘尖发出的劲。（图4-11）

Push outward with the elbow adhering to your opponent's limbs or push with the tip of the elbow. (Fig. 4-11)

图 4-11　肘
Fig. 4-11　Zhou (Elbowing)

8. 靠 Kao (Leaning)

通过肩、背、胯、胸等身体部位向外靠打发放的挤推之劲。（图4-12）

The force of squeezing and pushing is accumulated through the movements of pushing shoulder, back, crotch, chest and other parts of the body outward. (Fig. 4-12)

图 4-12 靠
Fig. 4-12 Kao (Leaning)

二、步 法　　　　　　　Step Techniques

太极拳的步法要求轻灵沉稳，虚实分明，两脚移动时轻起轻落，迈步如猫行，由点及面，重心稳定。在步法转换中，落脚的位置（距离、宽度、方向）要适当，脚尖或脚跟辗转的角度要适度，支撑腿要保持平稳，身体重心不可忽起忽落，移动腿要屈伸灵活，不可僵硬。

The footwork of Taijiquan should be light and steady, making a clear distinction between emptiness and solidness. When the feet move, they rise and fall lightly. The step moves like a cat. From point to surface, the center of weight is stable. In the step change, perfom a proper position of the foot (distance, width, direction) ; the angle of the toes or heels should be moderate; the supporting legs should be stable; the body's center of weight should not rise or fall, and the moving legs should be flexible and not stiff.

1. 上步　　　　　　　Stepping Forward

一腿支撑，另一腿提起经支撑腿内侧向前上步，脚跟先着地，随着重心前移，全脚着地。（图4-13）

One leg is maintained for support, with the other leg lifted and stepping forward through the inner side of the supporting leg; the heel touches the ground first, and then the whole foot follows up as the center of weight moves forward. (Fig. 4-13)

图 4-13　上步
Fig. 4-13 Stepping forward

2. 退步   Stepping Backward

一腿支撑，另一腿提起后退一步，前脚掌先着地随着重心后移，全脚着地。（图4-14）

One leg is maintained for support, with the other leg lifted up and stepping back; the forefoot touches the ground first, and the whole foot follows up as the center of weight moves backward. (Fig. 4-14)

图 4-14　退步
Fig. 4-14 Stepping backward

3. 侧行步   Side Step

　　一腿支撑，另一腿侧向开步，前脚掌先着地，随着重心横移，全脚着地逐渐过渡为支撑腿；另一腿提起，向支撑腿内侧收步，仍须先以前脚掌着地，随着重心横移，全脚着地过渡为支撑腿，收步时两脚间距为10～20厘米。（图4-15）

One leg supports the body, and the other leg moves sideways; the forefoot touches the ground first, and as the center of weight moves horizontally, the whole foot touches the ground and gradually changes into the supporting leg; the other leg is lifted, and the step is retracted to the inside of the supporting leg, with the forefoot touching the ground first. As the center of weight shifts horizontally, the whole foot will be on the ground and change into a supporting leg, and the distance between the two feet when retracting is 10-20 cm. (Fig. 4-15)

图 4-15　侧行步
Fig. 4-15　Side step

三、腿　法　　　　　　　　　　　　Leg Techniques

1.蹬脚　　　　　　　　　　　　　　　Kicking with Heel

支撑腿微屈，另一腿屈膝提起，脚尖上翘，以脚跟为力点蹬出，腿自然伸直，勿低于水平位；蹬伸腿一定要先屈后伸，不可直腿上摆；做蹬脚时，支撑腿要稳定，上体保持中正，不可前俯后仰，左右歪斜。（图4-16）

The supporting leg is slightly bent, and the other leg is bent and raised; the toes are upturned, and the heel is used as the force point to push out. The leg should be straightened naturally, not lower than the horizontal position; when pushing the leg, be sure to bend first and then extend without straightening the leg up; when you are kicking, the supporting leg should be stable, and the upper body should be kept upright instead of falling forward or backward and skewing sideways. (Fig. 4-16)

图 4-16　蹬脚
Fig. 4-16 Kicking with heal

2. 分脚 Kicking with Instep

支撑腿微屈，另一腿屈膝提起，然后小腿上摆弹踢，腿自然伸直，脚面展平，上举腿勿低于水平。（图4-17）

Slightly bend the supporting leg, and lift the other knee; then swing and flip the calf upwards. The leg should be straightened naturally and the instep should be flat. Do not raise the leg below the horizontal level. (Fig. 4-17)

图 4-17　分脚
Fig. 4-17　Kicking with instep

3. 拍脚 Smacking Feet

支撑腿微屈，另一腿脚面展平向上直摆，以同侧手或异侧手迎拍脚面；勿击拍落空，击响时摆动腿勿弯曲。（图4-18）

Slightly bend the supporting leg, flatten the instep of the other leg and swing it straight up; pat the instep with the same or opposite hand; do not miss the strike, or bend the swinging leg when making a clear sound. (Fig. 4-18)

图 4-18　拍脚
Fig. 4-18 Smacking feet

4. 摆莲脚　　　　　　　　　　　　　　　　　　　　　　　　　Lotus Kick

支撑腿微屈，另一腿从异侧经胸前向外做扇形摆动，脚面展平，两手在体前依次击拍脚面，须两响，勿击拍落空，摆莲脚幅度勿过小。（图4-19）

The supporting leg is slightly bent, and the other leg swings outward from the opposite side through the chest following an arc; the instep is flattened, and the two hands pat the instep one by one in front of the body with two beeps. Don't miss the strike, or swing the lotus feet slightly. (Fig. 4-19)

图 4-19　摆莲脚
Fig. 4-19 Lotus kick

四、身　法　　　　　　　　　　　　　Body Techniques

太极拳的身法要求：以腰为轴，带动四肢；上下相随，圆活完整；中正安舒，无过不及；保持不偏不倚，旋转松活，自然平稳，上悬下沉，中节舒松；动作上下完整贯穿，不可僵滞浮软、俯仰歪斜，应轻灵沉稳、平和自然。

Take the waist as the axis and move the limbs. The upper and lower parts of the body are coordinated, smooth, and flexible. They should maintain a comfortable position. The body should be upright, relaxed, flexible in rotation, naturally stable with the head pulled up, feet grasping the ground slightly and the middle part relaxed and comfortable. The movement is smooth, complete, stable, peaceful and natural without any letup, stiffness, swing, or obliqueness.

五、眼　法　　　　　　　　　　　　　　Eye Techniques

太极拳的眼法要求：动作转换时眼随上手，动作到位，平视远望，往下的动作目视前下方；讲究"神聚于眼""神在眉宇之间"；精神贯注，意念引导，神态自然，意动神随和势动神随相结合，换势运转时眼睛要与手法、腿法、身法协调配合；练拳时对视野以内的人、物、景应视而不见，做到内外相合，神形一致；头领气沉有豪气，眼神与动作密切配合。

The eyes follow the hand when the action is changed. The movement should be standard. Look straightly forward and look at the front and bottom when taking a downward action. What matters most is that you should concentrate on your eyes and forehead. Keep your concentration and be guided by your mind. Both mind and posture are followed by the spirit. When changing positions, the eyes should coordinate with the techniques of hand, leg and body. When practicing Taijiquan, you should turn a blind eye to people, objects, and scenery within your vision, so that the inside and the outside are in harmony, and the spirit and form are coordinated. There is a vigor by pulling up the head and standing steadily, and eyes are closely matched with movements.

六、呼吸法 Breathing Techniques

　　太极拳的呼吸法要求深、长、细、匀，呼吸自然，逆腹式呼吸配合拳式动作。太极拳练习结合呼吸，可起到舒展筋骨、调和气血、畅通经络、增加内劲，以气催力、按摩内脏、消除淤血、促进血液循环等作用。开、起、升、屈、虚时须吸气，合、落、降、伸、实时须呼气，每个动作完成到位都要呼气下沉。这样有意识地调节呼吸来配合动作，有助于使动作更协调、劲力更完整、精神更贯注。口闭齿扣，舌抵上腭；精神集中，心平气和，气沉丹田，呼吸自然。

Taijiquan requires deep, long, smooth and even breathing. Breathing should be natural, combining inverse abdominal breathing with fist movements. Taijiquan exercises combined with breathing can stretch the muscles and bones, reconcile Qi and blood, unblock the meridians, increase internal strength, stimulate energy, massage the internal organs, eliminate congestion, and promote blood circulation. Inhale when you stretch, stand up, rise, bend and make an empty movement, and exhale when you drop, fall, descend, stretch, and make a solid movement.Exhale when completing a movement. In this way, consciously adjusting the breathing to matching the movements will help make them more coordinated, complete, and focused. The mouth is closed, the teeth are clasped, and the tongue is on the palate; be concentrated and calm with Qi gathering into Dantian with natural breath.

七、技击法   Attacking Techniques

太极拳的技击法要求太极拳械动作体现武术攻防本质属性，运用踢、打、摔、拿、掤、捋、挤、采、挒、肘、靠等技法及器械技法。太极拳是快慢相间、刚柔相济的拳术，以武术的技击动作为主要内容。太极拳技击将传统技击术与现代技击术相结合，使格斗最简单、最实用、最有效。上封眼下顶裆、中间穿心肘，擒拿手指弱胜强。招无定法，一招多用，视实战变化而定。想哪打哪，意到拳到，随机应变。周身无处不是拳，挨到何处何处击。

The movements and weapons used in Taijiquan should reflect the essential attribute of attack and defense in Wushu, such as kicking, hitting, wrestling, holding, warding off, rolling back, pressing, pushing, pulling down, splitting, elbowing, leaning, stroke and weapon techniques. Taijiquan is a boxing that combines rapidness with slowness, vigor with softness and takes the attacking techniques in Wushu as its main content. Taijiquan combines traditional and modern techniques to make fighting the simplest, most practical and effective. Taijiquan requires covering eyes, kicking the crotch, hitting the middle with elbow and conquering strength with weakness by catch-and-hold finger control. It is flexibe for you to hit whatever you want with the fist striking as soon as Yi (the mind) appears. Every part of the body can be used as a fist and it hits wherever it goes.

太极拳段前九级考评技术内容

A Nine-tier Pre-Duan Grading System for Taijiquan

太极拳段前一级 　　Taijiquan: Pre-Duan Level 1

太极拳段前一级
Taijiquan: Pre-
Duan Level 1

动作名称

预备势

1. 起势

2. 开合桩

3. 升降桩

4. 收势

Names of Actions

Preparatory Posture

1. Commencing Posture

2.Opening and Closing Zhuang

3. Raising and Falling Zhuang

4. Closing Posture

练习太极拳段前一级开始前行抱拳礼。

Before your practice, perform the palm-fist salute.

预备势   Preparatory Posture

并步站立。（图5-1）

要点：口闭齿扣，舌抵上腭；上悬下沉，中节舒松；精神集中，心平气和，呼吸自然。

Stand with your feet together. (Fig. 5-1)

Key points: The mouth is closed, and the tongue is pressed against the palate; the upper part hangs down, and the middle section is relaxed; be concentrated and calm with natural breath.

图 5-1　预备势
Fig. 5-1 Preparatory posture

1. 起势   Commencing Posture

开步站立，两臂前举，屈膝按掌。（图5-2）

要点：松胯微屈膝，左脚开步，平行步站立，两臂前举吸气，屈膝按掌呼气。

Stand with your feet apart, raise your arms forward, bend your knees and press your palms down. (Fig. 5-2)

Key points: Slightly bend the knees with loose hips, open the left foot, stand in parallel, lift both arms forward to inhale, and exhale while bending the knees and pressing the palms down.

图 5-2　起势
Fig. 5-2 Commencing posture

2.开合桩   Opening and Closing Zhuang

两手分托，屈膝抱掌；两手分开，屈膝合抱。（图5-3）

要点：两手分托直立吸气，屈膝抱掌呼气；两手分开直立吸气，屈膝合抱呼气。

Hold your hands apart, bend your knees and embrace your palms; spread your hands apart, and bend your knees together. (Fig. 5-3)

Key points: Stand upright with both hands apart to inhale, bend your knees and embrace your palms to exhale; inhale when you stand upright with your hands apart, and exhale when you bend your knees and hug.

图 5-3　开合桩
Fig. 5-3 Opening and closing zhuang

3. 升降桩   Raising and Falling Zhuang

两手分托，屈膝抱掌；屈膝下蹲，屈膝上起。（图5-4）

要点：两手分托直立吸气，屈膝抱掌呼气；抱掌屈蹲呼气，慢起吸气。

Hold your hands apart, bend your knees and embrace your palms; bend your knees to squat, and bend your knees rising up. (Fig. 5-4)

Key points: Stand upright with both hands apart to inhale, bend your knees and embrace your palms to exhale; exhale when you squat with your palms folded, and inhale when you slowly rise.

图 5-4　升降桩
Fig. 5-4 Raising and falling zhuang

4. 收势 Closing Posture

屈蹲举臂，按掌直立，收脚并步。（图5-5）

要点：屈蹲举臂吸气，按落掌直立呼气，中正圆活，轻灵沉稳，平和自然，无过不及。

Bend and squat, raise your arms, press your palms down and stand upright; stand with your feet together. (Fig. 5-5)

Key points: Inhale when squatting and raising arms, and exhale when pressing down palms and standing upright. Keep movements smooth, flexible, lively, light, stable, peaceful and natural without excess and deficiency.

图 5-5 收势
Fig. 5-5 Closing posture

练习太极拳段前一级结束后行抱拳礼。

At the end of your practice, perform the palm-fist salute.

太极拳段前二级　　　　Taijiquan: Pre-Duan Level 2

太极拳段前二级
Taijiquan: Pre-
Duan Level 2

动作名称

预备势

1. 起势

2. 左右卷肱势

3. 收势

Names of Actions

Preparatory Posture

1. Commencing Posture

2. Zuoyou Juanhongshi (Forearm Rolling on both Sides)

3. Closing Posture

练习太极拳段前二级开始前行抱拳礼。

Before your practice, perform the palm-fist salute.

并步站立。（图5-6）

要点：口闭齿扣，舌抵上腭；上悬下沉，中节舒松；精神集中，心平气和，呼吸自然。

Stand with your feet together. (Fig. 5-6)

Key points: The mouth is closed, and the tongue is pressed against the palate; the upper part hangs down, and the middle section is relaxed; be concentrated and calm with natural breath.

图 5-6　预备势
Fig. 5-6 Preparatory posture

1. 起势   Commencing Posture

开步站立，两臂前举，屈膝按掌。（图5-7）

要点：松胯微屈膝，左脚开步，平行步站立，两臂前举吸气，屈膝按掌呼气。

Stand with your feet apart, raise your arms forward, bend your knees and press your palms down. (Fig. 5-7)

Key points: Slightly bend the knees with loose hips, open the left foot, stand in parallel, lift both arms forward to inhale, and exhale while bending the knees and pressing the palms down.

图 5-7 起势
Fig. 5-7 Commencing posture

2. 左右卷肱势   Zuoyou Juanhongshi (Forearm Rolling on both Sides)

转体举掌，收掌前推；反方向转体举掌，收掌前推。（图5-8）

要点：转体举掌吸气，收掌前推呼气；推掌顶肘劲力要沉实顺达。

Turn your body to raise your palms and push your palms forward; turn your body to raise your palms in the opposite direction and push your palms forward. (Fig. 5-8)

Key points: Turn your body and raise your palms to inhale; take back your palms and push forward to exhale; push your palms and elbows firmly and smoothly.

图 5-8　左右卷肱势
Fig. 5-8　Zuoyou Juanhongshi(Forearm Rolling on both Sides)

3. 收势　　　　　　　　　　　　　　　　　　　　Closing Posture

屈蹲举臂，按掌直立，收脚并步。（图5-9）

要点：屈蹲举臂吸气，按落掌直立呼气，中正圆活，轻灵沉稳，平和自然，无过不及。

Bend and squat; raise your arms; press your palms down and stand upright; stand with your feet together. (Fig. 5-9)

Key points: Inhale when squatting and raising arms, and exhale when pressing down palms and standing upright. Keep movements smooth, flexible, lively, light, stable, peaceful and natural without excess and deficiency.

图 5-9　收势
Fig. 5-9　Closing posture

练习太极拳段前二级结束后行抱拳礼。

At the end of your practice, perform the palm-fist salute.

太极拳段前三级   Taijiquan: Pre-Duan Level 3

太极拳段前三级
Taijiquan: Pre-
Duan Level 3

动作名称

预备势

1. 起势

2. 左右手挥琵琶

3. 收势

Names of Actions

Preparatory Posture

1. Commencing Posture

2. Zuoyou Shouhuipipa (Hands Playing the Lute on both Sides)

3. Closing Posture

练习太极拳段前三级开始前行抱拳礼。

Before your practice, perform the palm-fist salute.

并步站立。（图5-10）

要点：口闭齿扣，舌抵上腭；上悬下沉，中节舒松；精神集中，心平气和，呼吸自然。

Stand with your feet together. (Fig. 5-10)

Key points: The mouth is closed, and the tonque is pressed against the palate; the head is pulled up and the lower part is stable with the middle section relaxed; be concentrated and calm with natural breath.

图 5-10　预备势
Fig. 5-10 Preparatory posture

1. 起势   Commencing Posture

开步站立，两臂前举，屈膝按掌。（图5-11）

要点：松胯微屈膝，左脚开步，平行步站立，两臂前举吸气，屈膝按掌呼气。

Stand with your feet apart, raise your arms forward, bend your knees and press your palms down. (Fig. 5-11)

Key points: Slightly bend the knees with loose hips, open the left foot, stand in parallel, lift both arms forward to inhale, and exhale while bending the knees and pressing the palms down.

图 5-11　起势
Fig. 5-11 Commencing posture

2. 左右手挥琵琶 Zuoyou Shouhuipipa
(Hands Playing the Lute on both Sides)

转体摆掌，虚步合掌；反方向转体摆掌，虚步合掌。（图5-12）

要点：转体摆掌吸气，虚步合掌呼气；虚步与合掌协调配合。

Turn your body and swing your palms; bring your palms together with an empty step; turn your body and swing your palms in the opposite direction, and bring your palms together with an empty step. (Fig. 5-12)

Key points: Turn your body and swing your palms to inhale, then bring your palms together to exhale with an empty step; the empty step and the palms are coordinated.

图 5-12　左右手挥琵琶
Fig. 5-12 Zuoyou shouhuipipa (Hands playing the lute on both sides)

3. 收势   Closing Posture

屈蹲举臂，按掌直立，收脚并步。（图5-13）

要点： 屈蹲举臂吸气，按落掌直立呼气，中正圆活，轻灵沉稳，平和自然，无过不及。

Bend and squat; raise your arms; press your palms down and stand upright; stand with your feet together. (Fig. 5-13)

Key points: Inhale when squatting and raising arms, and exhale when pressing down palms to and standing upright. Keep movements smooth, flexible, lively, light, stable, peaceful and natural without excess and deficiency.

图 5-13　收势
Fig. 5-13 Closing posture

练习太极拳段前三级结束后行抱拳礼。

At the end of your practice, perform the palm-fist salute.

太极拳段前四级　　　　　Taijiquan: Pre-Duan Level 4

太极拳段前四级
Taijiquan: Pre-
Duan Level 4

动作名称

预备势

1. 起势

2. 左右白鹤亮翅

3. 收势

Names of Actions

Preparatory Posture

1. Commencing Posture

2. Zuoyou Baiheliangchi(White Crane Spreading Its Wings on both Sides)

3. Closing Posture

练习太极拳段前四级开始前行抱拳礼。

Before your practice, perform the palm-fist salute.

预备势   Preparatory Posture

并步站立。（图5-14）

要点：口闭齿扣，舌抵上腭；上悬下沉，中节舒松；精神集中，心平气和，呼吸自然。

Stand with your feet together. (Fig. 5-14)

Key points: The mouth is closed, and the tongue is pressed against the palate; the head is pulled up and the lower part is stable with the middle section relaxed; be concentrated and calm with natural breath.

图 5-14　预备势
Fig. 5-14 Preparatory posture

1. 起势   Commencing Posture

开步站立，两臂前举，屈膝按掌。（图5-15）

要点：松胯微屈膝，左脚开步，平行步站立，两臂前举吸气，屈膝按掌呼气。

Stand with your feet apart, raise your arms forward, bend your knees and press your palms down. (Fig. 5-15)

Key points: Slightly bend the knees with loose hips, open the left foot, stand in parallel, lift both arms forward to inhale, and exhale while bending the knees and pressing the palms down.

图 5-15　起势
Fig. 5-15 Commencing posture

2. 左右白鹤亮翅
Zuoyou Baiheliangchi
(White Crane Spreading Its Wings on both Sides)

退步抱掌，虚步挑掌；反方向退步抱掌，虚步合掌。（图5-16）

要点：退步抱掌吸气，虚步挑掌呼气；虚步与挑掌协调配合。

Retreat and hold the palms, then raise the palms with an empty step; hold the palms with a step backwards, and bring the palms together with an empty step in the opposite direction. (Fig. 5-16)

Key points: Step back, hold your palms and inhale; exhale with the palms raised in an empty step; coordinate the palms with the empty step.

图 5-16　左右白鹤亮翅
Fig. 5-16 Zuoyou baiheliangchi (White crane spreading its wings on both sides)

3. 收势   Closing Posture

屈蹲举臂，按掌直立，收脚并步。（图5-17）

要点：屈蹲举臂吸气，按落掌直立呼气，中正圆活，轻灵沉稳，平和自然，无过不及。

Bend and squat; raise your arms; press your palms down and stand upright; stand with your feet together. (Fig. 5-17)

Key points: Inhale when squatting and raising arms, and exhale when pressing down palms and standing upright. Keep movements smooth, flexible, lively, light, stable, peaceful and natural without excess and deficiency.

图 5-17　收势
Fig. 5-17 Closing posture

练习太极拳段前四级结束后行抱拳礼。

At the end of your practice, perform the palm-fist salute.

太极拳段前五级　　　　Taijiquan: Pre-Duan Level 5

太极拳段前五级
Taijiquan: Pre-
Duan Level 5

动作名称

预备势

1. 起势

2. 左右搂膝拗步

3. 收势

Names of Actions

Preparatory Posture

1. Commencing Posture

2. Zuoyou Louxi'aobu (Brushing Knees and Twisting Steps on both Sides)

3. Closing Posture

练习太极拳段前五级开始前行抱拳礼。

Before your practice, perform the palm-fist salute.

预备势   Preparatory Posture

并步站立。（图5-18）

要点：口闭齿扣，舌抵上腭；上悬下沉，中节舒松；精神集中，心平气和，呼吸自然。

Stand with your feet together. (Fig. 5-18)

Key points: The mouth is closed, and the tongue is pressed against the palate; the head is pulled up and the lower part is stable with the middle section relaxed; be concentrated and calm with natural breath.

图 5-18　预备势
Fig. 5-18 Preparatory posture

1. 起势　　　　　　　　　　　　　　　　　Commencing Posture

开步站立，两臂前举，屈膝按掌。（图5-19）

要点： 松胯微屈膝，左脚开步，平行步站立，两臂前举吸气，屈膝按掌呼气。

Stand with your feet apart, raise your arms forward, bend your knees and press your palms down. (Fig. 5-19)

Key points: Slightly bend the knees with loose hips, open the left foot, stand in parallel, inhale while raising arms forward, and exhale while bending the knees and pressing the palms down.

图 5-19　起势
Fig. 5-19 Commencing posture

2. 左右搂膝拗步   Zuoyou Louxi'aobu (Brushing Knees and Twisting Steps on both Sides)

收脚举掌，弓步搂推；反方向收脚举掌，弓步搂推。（图5-20）

要点：收脚举掌吸气，弓步搂推呼气，以腰为轴，屈膝、松胯、转腰、蹬腿成弓步；推掌的腕与肩平，搂按掌至胯旁，注意松紧、虚实变化。

Retract the feet and raise the palms, brushing aside and pushing hands with bow steps; retract the feet and raise the palms in the opposite direction, brushing aside and pushing hands with bow step. (Fig. 5-20)

Key points: Retract the feet and raise the palms to inhale; brush aside and push hands with bow steps to exhale; with the waist as the axis bend the knees, relax the hips, turn the waist, and push the legs into a bow step; make the wrists of the palms pushed and the shoulders maintain a horizontal level, press the palms down to the crotch, and pay attention to the change of tightness and relaxation, emptiness and solidness.

图 5-20 左右搂膝拗步

Fig. 5-20 Zuoyou louxi'aobu (Brushing knees and twisting steps on both sides)

3. 收势   Closing Posture

屈蹲举臂，按掌直立，收脚并步。（图5-21）

要点： 屈蹲举臂吸气，按落掌直立呼气，中正圆活，轻灵沉稳，平和自然，无过不及。

Bend and squat; raise your arms; press down your palms and stand upright; stand with your feet together. (Fig. 5-21)

Key points: Inhale when squatting and raising arms, and exhale when pressing down palms and standing upright. Keep movements smooth, flexible, lively, light, stable, peaceful and natural without excess and deficiency.

图 5-21　收势
Fig. 5-21 Closing posture

练习太极拳段前五级结束后行抱拳礼。

At the end of your practice, perform the palm-fist salute.

太极拳段前六级   Taijiquan: Pre-Duan Level 6

太极拳段前六级
Taijiquan: Pre–
Duan Level 6

动作名称

预备势

1. 起势

2. 左右野马分鬃

3. 左右穿心肘

4. 收势

Names of the Actions

Preparatory Posture

1. Commencing Posture

2. Zuoyou Yemafenzong (Parting the Wild Horse's Mane on both Sides)

3. Zuoyou Chuanxinzhou (Penetrating Elbow on both Sides)

4. Closing Posture

练习太极拳段前六级开始前行抱拳礼。

Before your practice, perform the palm-fist salute.

<table>
<tr><td>预备势</td><td>Preparatory Posture</td></tr>
</table>

并步站立。（图5-22）

要点：口闭齿扣，舌抵上腭；上悬下沉，中节舒松；精神集中，心平气和，呼吸自然。

Stand with your feet together. (Fig. 5-22)

Key points: The mouth is closed, and the tongue is pressed against the palate; the head is pulled up and the lower part is stable with the middle section relaxed; be concentrated and calm with natural breath.

图 5-22　预备势
Fig. 5-22　Preparatory posture

1. 起势   Commencing Posture

开步站立，两臂前举，屈膝按掌。（图5-23）

要点：松胯微屈膝，左脚开步，平行步站立，两臂前举吸气，屈膝按掌呼气。

Stand with your feet apart, raise your arms forward, bend your knees and press your palms down. (Fig. 5-23)

Key points: Slightly bend the knees with loose hips, open the left foot, stand in parallel, inhale while raising arms forward, and exhale while bending the knees and pressing the palms down.

图 5-23　起势
Fig. 5-23 Commencing posture

2. 左右野马分鬃
Zuoyou Yemafenzong
(Parting the Wild Horse's Mane on both Sides)

收脚抱掌，弓步分掌；反方向收脚抱掌，弓步分掌。（图5-24）

要点：收脚抱掌吸气，弓步分掌呼气，弓步与分掌协调配合。

Make a ball-holding gesture when moving back your feet, and seperate hands when making a bow stance; repeat the movement in the opposite direction. (Fig. 5-24)

Key points: Inhale when making a ball-holding gesture and moving back your feet; exhale when separating hands with a bow stance; coordinate the bow stance with seperated hands.

图 5-24　左右野马分鬃
Fig. 5-24　Zuoyou yemafenzong (Parting the wild horse's mane on both sides)

3. 左右穿心肘

Zuoyou Chuanxinzhou
(Penetrating Elbow on both Sides)

右转伸掌，马步顶肘；左转伸掌，马步顶肘。（图5-25）

要点：转体伸掌吸气，马步顶肘呼气；腰胯运转，顶肘发劲，力达肘尖，快慢相间，刚柔相济。

Turn right, stretch your palm and push your elbow with a horse stance; turn left, stretch your palm and push your elbow with a horse stance. (Fig. 5-25)

Key points: Inhale when turning around and stretching out your palms and exhale when pushing your elbow with a horse stance; the waist and hips rotate and the elbow pushes with force to make the force reach the elbow's tip. Pay attention to the combination of rapidness and slowness, vigor and softness.

图 5-25　左右穿心肘
Fig. 5-25 Zuoyou chuanxinzhou (Penetrating elbow on both sides)

4. 收势   Closing Posture

屈蹲举臂，按掌直立，收脚并步。（图5-26）

要点：屈蹲举臂吸气，按落掌直立呼气，中正圆活，轻灵沉稳，平和自然，无过不及。

Bend and squat; raise your arms; press down your palms and stand upright; stand with your feet together. (Fig. 5-26)

Key points: Inhale when squatting and raising arms, and exhale when pressing down palms and standing upright. Keep movements smooth, flexible, lively, light, stable, peaceful and natural without excess and deficiency.

图 5-26 收势
Fig. 5-26 Closing posture

练习太极拳段前六级结束后行抱拳礼。

At the end of your practice, perform the palm-fist salute.

太极拳段前七级 Taijiquan: Pre-Duan Level 7

太极拳段前七级
Taijiquan: Pre-
Duan Level 7

动作名称

预备势

1. 起势

2. 左右单鞭

3. 左右穿掌下势

4. 收势

Names of Actions

Preparatory Posture

1. Commencing Posture

2. Zuoyou Danbian (Single Whip on both Sides)

3. Zuoyou Chuanzhangxiashi (Puncturing Palm on both Sides)

4. Closing Posture

练习太极拳段前七级开始前行抱拳礼。

Before your practice, perform the palm-fist salute.

并步站立。（图5-27）

要点：口闭齿扣，舌抵上腭；上悬下沉，中节舒松；精神集中，心平气和，呼吸自然。

Stand with your feet together. (Fig. 5-27)

Key points: The mouth is closed, and the tongue is pressed against the palate; the head is pulled up and the lower part is stable with the middle section relaxed; be concentrated and calm with natural breath.

图 5-27　预备势
Fig. 5-27 Preparatory posture

1. 起势 {Commencing Posture}

开步站立，两臂前举，屈膝按掌。（图5-28）

要点：松胯微屈膝，左脚开步，平行步站立，两臂前举吸气，屈膝按掌呼气。

Stand with your feet apart, raise your arms forward, bend your knees and press your palms down. (Fig. 5-28)

Key points: Slightly bend the knees with loose hips, open the left foot, stand in parallel, inhale while raising arms forward, and exhale while bending the knees and pressing the palms down.

图 5-28　起势
Fig. 5-28 Commencing posture

2. 左右单鞭　　　　　　Zuoyou Danbian (Single Whip on both Sides)

右勾手上步，弓步推掌；左勾手上步，弓步推掌。（图5-29）

要点：上步吸气，弓步推掌呼气；弓步时前腿膝关节垂直于脚面，不超出脚尖，脚跟踏实；弓步与推掌协调一致。

Step with the right hook and push the palm with a bow step; step on the left hook and push the palm with a bow step. (Fig. 5-29)

Key points: Inhale in the advancing step, push the palm in a bow step and exhale; when performing the bow step, the knee joint of the front leg is perpendicular to the instep, not beyond the toe, and the heel is stable; the bow step is coordinated with the pushing palm.

图 5-29　左右单鞭
Fig. 5-29 Zuoyou danbian (Single whip on both sides)

3. 左右穿掌下势

Zuoyou Chuanzhangxiashi
(Puncturing Palm on both Sides)

右弓步举掌，仆步穿掌；左弓步举掌，仆步穿掌。（图5-30）

要点：弓步举掌吸气，仆步穿掌呼气；仆步穿掌时，上体不要前俯；仆步屈蹲腿全蹲，平铺腿伸直，全脚掌内扣着地。

Raise the palm with the right bow step and slide palm with a crouching step; raise the palm with the left bow step and slide palm with a crouching step. (Fig. 5-30)

Key points: Inhale when raising the palm with a bow step and exhale when sliding the palm with a crouching step; don't lean your upper body forward when sliding the palm in a croching step; bend the squatting legs, squat fully, straighten the tiled legs, and buckle the whole soles of the feel to the ground.

图 5-30　左右穿掌下势
Fig. 5-30 Zuoyou chuanzhangxiashi (Puncturing palm on both sides)

4. 收势   Closing Posture

屈蹲举臂，按掌直立，收脚并步。（图5-31）

要点： 屈蹲举臂吸气，按落掌直立呼气，中正圆活，轻灵沉稳，平和自然，无过不及。

Bend and squat; raise your arms; press down your palms and stand upright; stand with your feet together. (Fig. 5-31)

Key points: Inhale when squatting and raising arms, and exhale when pressing down palms and standing upright. Keep movements smooth, flexible, lively, light, stable, peaceful and natural without excess and deficiency.

图 5-31　收势
Fig. 5-31 Closing posture

练习太极拳段前七级结束后行抱拳礼。

At the end of your practice, perform the palm-fist salute.

太极拳段前八级 Taijiquan: Pre-Duan Level 8

动作名称

预备势

1. 起势

2. 左右白猿献果

3. 左右蹬脚

4. 收势

Names of Actions

Preparatory Posture

1. Commencing Posture

2. Zuoyou Baiyuanxianguo (White Ape Presenting Fruit on both Sides)

3. Heel Kick on both Sides

4. Closing Posture

练习太极拳段前八级开始前行抱拳礼。

Before your practice, perform the palm-fist salute.

并步站立。（图5-32）

要点：口闭齿扣，舌抵上腭；上悬下沉，中节舒松；精神集中，心平气和，呼吸自然。

Stand with your feet together. (Fig. 5-32)

Key points: The mouth is closed, and the tongue is pressed against the palate; the head is pulled up and the lower part is stable with the middle section relaxed; be concentrated and calm with natural breath.

图 5-32　预备势
Fig. 5-32 Preparatory posture

1. 起势   Commencing Posture

开步站立，两臂前举，屈膝按掌。（图5-33）

要点：松胯微屈膝，左脚开步，平行步站立，两臂前举吸气，屈膝按掌呼气。

Stand with your feet apart, raise your arms forward, bend your knees and press down your palms. (Fig. 5-33)

Key points: Slightly bend the knees with loose hips, open the left foot, stand in parallel, inhale while raising arms forward, and exhale while bending the knees and pressing the palms down.

图 5-33　起势
Fig. 5-33 Commencing posture

2. 左右白猿献果　　　　　　　　　　Zuoyou Baiyuanxianguo
(White Ape Presenting Fruit on both Sides)

收脚按掌，独立冲拳；落脚按掌，独立冲拳。（图5-34）

要点：提膝独立与上冲拳协调一致。

Move back the feet and press the palm down to punch the fist on one leg; press the palm down while dropping the foot and then punch the fist on one leg. (Fig. 5-34)

Key points: Knee-lifting-on-one-leg standing and upper punching are coordinated.

图 5-34　左右白猿献果

Fig. 5-34 Zuoyou baiyuanxianguo (White ape presenting fruit on both sides)

3. 左右蹬脚   Heel Kick on both Sides

落脚分掌，蹬脚分掌；反方向落脚分掌，蹬脚分掌。（图5-35）

要点： 身体不可前俯后仰。蹬脚时，上举腿要伸直，蹬脚不低于水平位，分掌和蹬脚动作协调一致。

Drop the feet and separate the palms, kick the foot and separate the palms; perform the same action in the opposite direction. (Fig. 5-35)

Key points: The body should not be bent forward or backward. when kicking, the leg should be straightened up, not lower than the horizontal position. The movement of separating the palm and kicking should be coordinated.

图 5-35　左右蹬脚
Fig. 5-35 Heel kick on both sides

4. 收势   Closing Posture

屈蹲举臂，按掌直立，收脚并步。（图5-36）

要点：屈蹲举臂吸气，按落掌直立呼气，中正圆活，轻灵沉稳，平和自然，无过不及。

Bend and squat; raise your arms; press down your palms and stand upright; stand with your feet together. (Fig. 5-36)

Key points: Inhale when squatting and raising arms, and exhale when pressing down palms and standing upright. Keep movements smooth, flexible, lively, light, stable, peaceful and natural without excess and deficiency.

图 5-36　收势
Fig. 5-36 Closing posture

练习太极拳段前八级结束后行抱拳礼。

At the end of your practice, perform the palm-fist salute.

太极拳段前九级　　Taijiquan: Pre-Duan Level 9

太极拳段前九级
Taijiquan: Pre-
Duan Level 9

动作名称

预备势

1. 起势

2. 左右揽雀尾

3. 十字手

4. 收势

Names of Actions

Preparatory Posture

1. Commencing Posture

2. Zuoyou Lanquewei (Grasping the Peacock's Tail on both Sides)

3. Shizishou (Cross Arms)

4. Closing Posture

练习太极拳段前九级开始前行抱拳礼。

Before your practice, perform the palm-fist salute.

预备势 Preparatory Posture

并步站立。（图5-37）

要点：口闭齿扣，舌抵上腭；上悬下沉，中节舒松；精神集中，心平气和，呼吸自然。

Stand with your feet together. (Fig. 5-37)

Key points: The mouth is closed, and the tongue is pressed against the palate; the head is pulled up and the lower part is stable with the middle section relaxed; be concentrated and calm with natural breath.

图 5-37　预备势
Fig. 5-37 Preparatory posture

1. 起势   Commencing Posture

开步站立，两臂前举，屈膝按掌。（图5-38）

要点：松胯微屈膝，左脚开步，平行步站立，两臂前举吸气，屈膝按掌呼气。

Stand with your feet apart, raise your arms forward, bend your knees and press down your palms. (Fig. 5-38)

Key points: Slightly bend the knees with loose hips, open the left foot, stand in parallel, inhale while raising arms forward, and exhale while bending the knees and pressing down the palms.

图 5-38　起势
Fig. 5-38 Commencing posture

2. 左右揽雀尾

Zuoyou Lanquewei
(Grasping the Peacock's Tail on both Sides)

收脚抱掌，弓步前掤，转体下捋，弓步前挤，后坐下按，弓步按推；反方向收脚抱掌，弓步前掤，转体下捋，弓步前挤，后坐下按，弓步按推。（图5-39）

要点： 弓步掤臂呈弧形，腕与肩平；两手下捋沿弧线运行，下捋时重心后移，两腿虚实分明，上体保持中正；弓步前挤时两臂向前撑圆；两掌按推，两臂沿立圆运行；弓步与掤臂、前挤、按推协调配合。

Move back your feet and make a ball-holding gesture; push forward in a bow step; turn your body and pull down palms; push forward in a bow step; sit down and press down palms; push in a bow step. Repeat these movements in the opposite direction. (Fig. 5-39)

Key points: In a bow step, ward off arms in a curve and maintain wrists and shoulders at the same height; the hands move along an arc when pressed down, and the body's center of weight moves backward; make a clear distincion between emptiness and solidness on the legs, and the upper body remains erect; press forward in a bow step and stretch two arms; push two palms forward, and the arms run along the circle; the bow step is coordinated the movements of warding-off, pushing and pressing arms.

图 5-39　左右揽雀尾
Fig. 5-39 Zuoyou lanquewei (Grasping the peacock's tail on both sides)

3. 十字手   Shizishou (Cross Arms)

弓步摆掌，开立抱掌。（图5-40）

要点：弓步摆掌吸气，开立抱掌呼气；平行步，两掌交叉十字合抱于体前，两臂保持弧形，圆满舒适，沉肩坠肘。

Swing your palms with a bow step and cross arms when standing apart. (Fig. 5-40)

Key points: Inhale when swinging palms in a bow step and exhale when crossing arms in a separate step; cross arms in front of the chest in a separate step; keep both arms in an arc, round and comfortable; sink your shoulders and drop your elbows.

图 5-40　十字手
Fig. 5-40　Shizishou (Cross arms)

4. 收势   Closing Posture

屈蹲举臂，按掌直立，收脚并步。（图5-41）

要点： 屈蹲举臂吸气，按落掌直立呼气，中正圆活，轻灵沉稳，平和自然，无过不及。

Bend and squat; raise your arms; press down your palms and stand upright; stand with your feet together. (Fig. 5-41)

Key points: Inhale when squatting and raising arms, and exhale when pressing down palms and standing upright. Keep movements smooth, flexible, lively ,light, stable, peaceful and natural without excess and deficiency.

图 5-41　收势
Fig. 5-41 Closing posture

练习太极拳段前九级结束后行抱拳礼。

At the end of your practice, perform the palm-fist salute.

太极拳段位
考评技术内容

Duanwei Grading System
for Taijiquan

一段太极拳 {Taijiquan: Grade 1}

动作名称

预备势

1. 起势
2. 卷肱势
3. 搂膝拗步
4. 野马分鬃
5. 云手
6. 金鸡独立
7. 蹬脚
8. 揽雀尾
9. 十字手
10. 收势

Names of Actions

Preparatory Posture

1. Commencing Posture
2. Juanhongshi (Forearm Rolling)
3. Louxi'aobu (Brushing Knees and Twisting Steps)
4. Yemafenzong (Parting the Wild Horse's Mane)
5. Yunshou (Waving Hands like Clouds)
6. Jinjiduli (Golden Cock Standing on One Leg)
7. Heel Kick
8. Lanquewei (Grasping the Peacock's Tail)
9. Shizishou (Cross Arms)
10. Closing Posture

一段太极拳
Taijiquan: Grade 1

练习一段太极拳开始前行抱拳礼。

Before your practice, perform the palm-fist salute.

并步站立。（图6-1）

要点：口闭齿扣，舌抵上腭；上悬下沉，中节舒松；精神集中，心平气和，呼吸自然。

Stand with your feet together. (Fig. 6-1)

Key points: The mouth is closed, and the tongue is pressed against the palate; the head is pulled up and the lower part is stable with the middle section relaxed; be concentrated and calm with natural breath.

图 6-1 并步站立
Fig. 6-1 Stand with your feet together

（1）开步站立。（图6-2）

Stand with your feet apart. (Fig. 6-2)

图 6-2　开步站立
Fig. 6-2 Stand with your feet apart

（2）两臂前举。（图6-3）

Raise your arms forward. (Fig. 6-3)

图 6-3　两臂前举
Fig. 6-3 Raise your arms forward

（3）屈蹲下按。（图6-4）

Bend your knees and press your palms down. (Fig. 6-4)

图 6-4　屈蹲下按
Fig. 6-4 Bend your knees and press your palms down

要点：身型要求松胯敛臀，含胸拔背，沉肩坠肘，虚领顶劲；下按掌掌指舒展，掌心微含；中正安舒，气沉丹田，松静自然。

Key points: Relax the crotch and clench the buttock, relax the chest and draw the back, sink the shoulders and drop the elbows, and pull up the head and relax the neck; press the palms down, stretch the palms and fingers, and the palms slightly shape a circle and maintain it; keep the body upright, calm and comfortable; gather Qi into Dantian and be relaxed, quiet and natural.

2.卷肱势　　　　　　　　　　　　　　　Juanhongshi (Forearm Rolling)

（1）转体举掌。（图6-5）

Turn the body and raise the palms. (Fig. 6-5)

图 6-5　转体举掌
Fig. 6-5 Turn the body and raise the palms

113

（2）收掌前推。（图6-6）

Move back the palm and push forward. (Fig. 6-6)

图6-6　收掌前推

Fig. 6-6　Move back the palm and push forward

（3）转体举掌。（图6-7）

Turn the body and raise the palms. (Fig. 6-7)

图6-7　转体举掌

Fig. 6-7　Turn the body and raise the palms

（4）收掌前推。（图6-8）

Move back the palm and push forward. (Fig. 6-8)

图 6-8　收掌前推
Fig. 6-8 Move back the palm and push forward

要点：推掌时，身体不可前俯后仰，要沉肩垂肘，坐腕舒掌；劲力要沉实顺达。

Key points: When pushing the palm, do not lean forward or backward, instead, sink your shoulders and drop your elbows, and slightly tighten the wrist and relax the palms. The strength should be steady and smooth.

3. 搂膝拗步　　Louxi'aobu (Brushing Knees and Twisting Steps)

（1）收脚举掌。（图6-9）

Move your feet back and raise your palms. (Fig. 6-9)

图 6-9　收脚举掌
Fig. 6-9 Move your feet back and raise your palms

（2）弓步搂推。（图6−10）

Brush aside and push the palm with a bow step. (Fig. 6-10)

图 6−10　弓步搂推
Fig. 6-10 Brush aside and push the palm with a bow step

（3）收脚举掌。（图6−11）

Move your feet back and raise your palms. (Fig. 6-11)

图 6−11　收脚举掌
Fig. 6-11 Move your feet back and raise your palms

（4）弓步搂推。（图6-12）

Brush aside and push your palm with a bow step. (Fig. 6-12)

图 6-12　弓步搂推
Fig. 6-12 Brush aside and palm with a bow step

要点：以腰为轴，弓步推掌时，沉肩坠肘，搂掌经膝前向上划弧搂按至胯旁；上步勿抬脚过高，膝关节与脚尖同向；重心前移、屈膝、松胯、转腰、蹬腿；弓步时前脚尖微内扣，前腿膝关节垂直于脚面但不超出脚尖，后腿离地，脚跟以脚掌为轴做后蹬调整；注意松紧虚实变化。

Key points: Take the waist as the axis, push the palm with a lunge, sink the shoulders and drop the elbows; the palm circles around the knee, and then raise it up in an arc and press it dowh to reach the hip; don't lift the foot too high when stepping forward. Your knee joint is in the same direction as your tiptoes. Move your body forward, bend your knees, relax your crotch, turn your waist and kick your leg; in the bow step, the front toes are slightly buckled inward; the knee joint of the front leg should be positioned between the instep and tiptoes; the rear leg should be off the ground, and the heel should be adjusted with the sole of the foot which is taken as the axis. Pay attention to the change of softness and tightness, emptiness and solidness.

4. 野马分鬃   Yemafenzong (Parting the Wild Horse's Mane)

（1）收脚抱掌。（图6-13）

Move back your feet and make a ball-holding gesture. (Fig. 6-13)

图 6-13   收脚抱掌

Fig. 6-13 Move back your feet and make a ball-holding gesture

（2）弓步分掌。（图6-14）

Separate the palms with a bow step. (Fig. 6-14)

图 6-14   弓步分掌

Fig. 6-14 Separate the palms with a bow step

（3）收脚抱掌。（图6-15）

Move back your feet and make a ball-holding gesture. (Fig. 6-15)

图 6-15　收脚抱掌
Fig. 6-15　Move back your feet and make a ball-holding gesture

（4）弓步分掌。（图6-16）

Separate the palms with a bow step. (Fig. 6-16)

图 6-16　弓步分掌
Fig. 6-16　Separate the palms with a bow step

要点：两臂分开时要经过两掌心相对。身体转动须以腰为轴，弓步动作与分掌协调一致；上下肢要协调配合，四肢勿与躯干脱节。

Key points: When the arms are separated, they must pass through the two palms and face each other. the body rotates with the waist as the axis, and the bow step is coordinated with the separate palms; the upper and lower limbs shall be coordinated, and so are the limbs and the trunk.

5. 云手   Yunshou (Waving Hands like Clouds)

（1）收步云掌。（图6–17）

Step back and wave your palms. (Fig. 6-17)

图 6–17　收步云掌

Fig. 6-17 Step back and wave your palms

（2）开步云掌。（图6–18）

Wave your palms with an open step. (Fig. 6-18)

图 6–18　开步云掌

Fig. 6-18 Wave your palms with an open step

（3）弓步举掌。（图6-19）

Raise your palms with a bow step. (Fig. 6-19)

图 6-19　弓步举掌
Fig. 6-19　Raise your palms with a bow step

（4）收步云掌。（图6-20）

Step back and wave your palms. (Fig. 6-20)

图 6-20　收步云掌
Fig. 6-20　Step back and wave your palms

（5）开步云掌。（图6-21）

Wave your palms with an open step. (Fig. 6-21)

图 6-21　开步云掌

Fig. 6-21 Wave your palms with an open step

（6）弓步举掌。（图6-22）

Raise your palms with a bow step. (Fig. 6-22)

图 6-22　弓步举掌

Fig. 6-22 Raise your palms with a bow step

要点：身体转动以腰为轴，带动两手在体前翻、转、拧、裹、立圆、云拨，手高不过眉；下肢移动时，身体重心稳定；眼的视线随上手而移动，眼神与动作要协调配合。

Key points: The body rotates with the waist as the axis, and is followed by two hands turning, twisting, drawing, circling and waving in front of the body. Two hands are at the same height as eye brows. When the lower limbs move, the body is stable. Eyes move with the upper hand and are coordinated with movements.

6. 金鸡独立   Jinjiduli (Golden Cock Standing on One Leg)

（1）翻手摆掌。（图6-23）

Flip your hands and wave your palms. (Fig. 6-23)

图 6-23 　翻手摆掌

Fig. 6-23　Flip your hands and wave your palms

（2）提膝挑掌。（图6-24）

Lift the knee and the palm (right). (Fig. 6-24)

图 6-24 　提膝挑掌

Fig. 6-24　Lift the knee and the palm (right)

（3）提膝挑掌。（图6-25）

Lift the knee and the palm(left). (Fig. 6-25)

图 6-25　提膝挑掌

Fig. 6-25 Lift the knee and the palm (left)

要点：两手一挑一按要与提膝动作协调一致。独立上提腿勿低于水平位，支撑腿微屈，上体正直。

Key points: The movements of lifting and pressing hands should be coordinated with the knee-lifting action. the position of the lifted leg should not be lower than the horizontal level; the supporting leg should be slightly bent, and the upper body should be upright.

7. 蹬脚   Heel Kick

（1）落脚合掌。（图6-26）

Drop your feet and bring your palms together. (Fig. 6-26)

图 6-26　落脚合掌

Fig. 6-26　Drop your feet and bring your palms together

（2）蹬脚分掌。（图6-27）

Kick and separate the palms. (Fig. 6-27)

图 6-27　蹬脚分掌

Fig. 6-27　Kick and separate the palms

（3）落脚合掌。（图6-28）

Drop your feet and bring your palms together. (Fig. 6-28)

图 6-28　落脚合掌
Fig. 6-28 Drop your feet and bring your palms together

（4）蹬脚分掌。（图6-29）

Kick and separate the palms. (Fig. 6-29)

图 6-29　蹬脚分掌
Fig. 6-29 Kick and separate the palms

要点：身体不可前俯后仰。蹬脚时，上举腿要伸直，蹬脚不低于水平位，分掌和蹬脚动作协调一致。

Key points: The body cannot be bent forward or backward. when kicking, the legs should be straightened up, and the position should not be lower than the horizontal level; the movement of separating the palms and kicking should be coordinated.

126

8. 揽雀尾　　　　　　　　　　　　Lanquewei (Grasping the Peacock's Tail)

（1）收脚抱掌。（图6-30）

Move back your feet and make a ball-holding gesture. (Fig. 6-30)

图 6-30　收脚抱掌

Fig. 6-30　Move back your feet and make a ball-holding gesture

（2）弓步前掤。（图6-31）

Ward off with a bow step. (Fig. 6-31)

图 6-31　弓步前掤

Fig. 6-31　Ward off with a bow step

（3）转体下捋。（图6-32）

Roll back and turn the body. (Fig. 6-32)

图 6-32　转体下捋
Fig. 6-32　Roll back and turn the body

（4）弓步前挤。（图6-33）

Press forward with a bow step. (Fig. 6-33)

图 6-33　弓步前挤
Fig. 6-33　Press forward with a bow step

（5）后坐下按。（图6-34）

Sit back and press down palms. (Fig. 6-34)

图 6-34　后坐下按

Fig. 6-34 Sit back and press down palms

（6）弓步按推。（图6-35）

Push your palms with a bow step. (Fig. 6-35)

图 6-35　弓步按推

Fig. 6-35 Push your palms with a bow step

（7）收脚抱掌。（图6-36）

Move back your feet and make a ball-holding gesture. (Fig. 6-36)

图 6-36　收脚抱掌

Fig. 6-36　Move back your feet and make a ball-holding gesture

（8）弓步前掤。（图6-37）

Ward off with a bow step. (Fig. 6-37)

图 6-37　弓步前掤

Fig. 6-37 Ward off with a bow step

（9）转体下捋。（图6-38）

Roll back and turn the body. (Fig. 6-38)

图 6-38　转体下捋
Fig. 6-38 Roll back and turn the body

（10）弓步前挤。（图6-39）

Press forward with a bow step. (Fig. 6-39)

图 6-39　弓步前挤
Fig. 6-39 Press forward with a bow step

（11）后坐下按。（图6-40）

Sit back and press down palms. (Fig. 6-40)

图 6-40　后坐下按
Fig. 6-40　Sit back and press down palms

（12）弓步按推。（图6-41）

Push your palms with a bow step. (Fig. 6-41)

图 6-41　弓步按推
Fig. 6-41　Push your palms with a bow step

　　要点：弓步掤臂呈弧形，腕与肩平；两手下捋沿弧线运行；下捋时重心后移，两腿虚实分明，上体保持中正；弓步前挤时两臂向前撑圆，两掌按推，两臂沿立圆运行；弓步与掤臂、前挤、按推协调配合。

Key points: Ward off the arms in an arc with a bow step and maintain wrists and shoulders at the same height; the hands move along the arc when pressed down and the center of weight moves backward; make a clear distinction between emptiness and solidness on the legs, and the upper body remains upright; push two arms forward, and make them run along the circle; the bow step is coordinated with the movements of the arms.

9. 十字手   Shizishou (Cross Arms)

弓步摆掌，开立抱掌。（图6-42）

Swing your palms with a bow step, and then make a ball-holding gesture with an open step. (Fig. 6-42)

图 6-42　十字手

Fig. 6-42　Shizishou (Cross arms)

要点： 平行步，两掌交叉十字合抱于体前，两臂保持弧形，圆满舒适，沉肩坠肘。

Key points: Cross your palms in front of your body in a parallel step; keep your arms in an arc, round and comfortable; sink your shoulders and drop your elbows.

10. 收势 Closing Posture

（1）翻掌分手。（图6-43）

Turn your palms over and separate your hands. (Fig. 6-43)

图 6-43　翻掌分手
Fig. 6-43 Turn your palms over and separate your hands

（2）垂臂按掌。（图6-44）

Drop your arms and press down your palms. (Fig. 6-44)

图 6-44　垂臂按掌
Fig. 6-44 Drop your arms and press down your palms

（3）收脚并步。（图6-45）

Move your feet back and stand with your feet together. (Fig. 6-45)

图 6-45　收脚并步

Fig. 6-45 Move your feet back and stand with your feet together

要点： 中正圆活，轻灵沉稳，平和自然，无过不及。

Key points: Keep movements smooth and lively, light and steady, peaceful and natural without excess and deficiency.

练习一段太极拳结束后行抱拳礼。

At the end of your practice, perform the palm-fist salute.

二段太极拳 　　　　　　　　　　　Taijiquan: Grade 2

动作名称

预备势

第一段

1. 起势
2. 左右野马分鬃
3. 白鹤亮翅
4. 左右搂膝拗步
5. 进步搬拦捶
6. 如封似闭
7. 单鞭
8. 手挥琵琶

第二段

9. 倒卷肱
10. 左右穿梭
11. 海底针
12. 闪通背
13. 云手
14. 左右揽雀尾
15. 十字手
16. 收势

Names of Actions

Preparatory Posture

The First Section

1. Commencing Posture

2. Zuoyou Yemafenzong (Parting the Wild Horse's Mane on both Sides)

3. Baiheliangchi (White Crane Spreading Its Wings)

4. Zuoyou Louxi'aobu (Brushing Knees and Twisting Steps on both Sides)

5. Jinbu Banlanchui (Stepping forward, Parrying, Blocking, and Punching)

6. Rufengsibi (Pushing one's Hands forward in Defence)

7. Danbian (Single Whip)

8. Shouhuipipa (Hand Playing the Lute)

The Second Section

9. Daojuanhong (Stepping back and Curling Arms)

10. Zuoyou Chuansuo (Moving the Shuttle on both Sides)

11. Haidizhen (Needle at the Bottom of the Sea)

12. Shantongbei (Deflecting through the Arms)

13. Yunshou (Waving Hands like Clouds)

14. Zuoyou Lanquewei (Grasping the Peacock's Tail on both Sides)

15. Shizishou (Cross Arms)

16. Closing Posture

二段太极拳
Taijiquan: Grade 2

练习二段太极拳开始前行抱拳礼。

Before your practice, perform the palm-fist salute.

预备势　　　　　　　　　　　　　　　　　　　　Preparatory Posture

并步站立。（图6-46）

要点：口闭齿扣，舌抵上腭；上悬下沉，中节舒松；精神集中，心平气和，呼吸自然。

Stand with your feet together. (Fig. 6-46)

Key points: The mouth is closed, and the tongue is pressed against the palate; the head is pulled up and the lower part is stable with the middle section relaxed; be concentrated and calm with natural breath.

图 6-46　并步站立
Fig. 6-46　Stand with your feet together

第一段   The First Section

1. 起势   Commencing Posture

（1）开步站立。（图6-47）

Stand with your feet apart. (Fig. 6-47)

图 6-47　开步站立
Fig. 6-47 Stand with your feet apart

（2）两臂前举。（图6-48）

Raise your arms forward. (Fig. 6-48)

图 6-48　两臂前举
Fig. 6-48 Raise your arms forward

（3）屈膝按掌。（图6-40）

Bend knees and press palms down. (Fig. 6-49)

图 6-49　屈膝按掌

Fig. 6-49　Bend knees and press palms down

要点：身型要求松胯敛臀，含胸拔背，沉肩坠肘，虚领顶劲；下按掌掌指舒展，掌心微含；中正安舒，气沉丹田，松静自然。

Key points: Relax the crotch and clench the buttock, relax the chest and draw the back, sink the shoulders and drop the elbows, and pull up the head and relax the neck; press the palms down, stretch the palms and fingers, and the palms slightly shape a circle and maintain it; keep the body upright, calm and comfortable; gather Qi into Dantian and be relaxed, quiet and natural.

2. 左右野马分鬃

Zuoyou Yemafenzong
(Parting the Wild Horse's Mane on both Sides)

（1）收脚抱掌。（图6-50）

Move back your feet and make a ball-holding gesture. (Fig. 6-50)

图 6-50　收脚抱掌

Fig. 6-50　Move back your feet and make a ball-holding gesture

（2）弓步分掌。（图6-51）

Separate palms with a bow step. (Fig. 6-51)

图 6-51　弓步分掌
Fig. 6-51　Separate palms with a bow step

（3）收脚抱掌。（图6-52）

Move back your feet and make a ball-holding gesture. (Fig. 6-52)

图 6-52　收脚抱掌
Fig. 6-52　Move back your feet and make a ball-holding gesture

（4）弓步分掌。（图6-53）

Separate palms with a bow step. (Fig. 6-53)

图 6-53　弓步分掌
Fig. 6-53　Separate palms with a bow step

要点：弓步斜分掌时两臂保持弧形，弓步与分掌协调配合；身体重心转换保持平稳，式正招圆，紧凑灵活。

Key points: When separating the palms with a bow step, the arms should be arc-shaped, and the bow step and the separation should be coordinated; the shift of the body's center of weight should be kept stable, and the body is upright; the movements should be smooth and flexible.

3. 白鹤亮翅　　　　　Baiheliangchi (White Crane Spreading Its Wings)

跟步抱掌，虚步挑掌。（图6-54）

Make a ball-holding gesture when moving one leg forward, and lift the palms with an empty step. (Fig. 6-54)

图 6-54　白鹤亮翅
Fig. 6-54 Baheliangchi (White crane spreading its wings)

要点：虚步时后脚脚跟踏实。虚步与挑掌、按掌协调配合，上下相随，虚实分明。

Key points: The heel is stable when making an empty step. the empty step is coordinated with the movements of lifting and pressing palms, the upper and lower parts of the body should be coordinated and make a clear distinction between emptiness and solidness.

4. 左右搂膝拗步

Zuoyou Louxi'aobu (Brushing Knees and Twisting Steps on both Sides)

（1）收脚举掌。（图6-55）

Move your feet back and raise your palms. (Fig. 6-55)

图 6-55　收脚举掌

Fig. 6-55 Move your feet back and raise your palms

（2）弓步搂推。（图6-56）

Brush aside and push the palm with a bow step. (Fig. 6-56)

图 6-56　弓步搂推

Fig. 6-56 Brush aside and push the palm with a bow step

（3）收脚举掌。（图6-57）

Move your feet back and raise your palms. (Fig. 6-57)

图 6-57　收脚举掌
Fig. 6-57 Move your feet back and raise your palms

（4）弓步搂推。（图6-58）

Brush aside and push the palm with a bow step. (Fig. 6-58)

图 6-58　弓步搂推
Fig. 6-58 Brush aside and push the palm with a bow step

要点：上步时脚跟不可拖地，不可抬得过高；移动时身体重心平稳；弓步与搂掌、推掌协调配合；中正安舒，动静有序。

Key points: When stepping forward, the heels should not be dragged or raised too high; the body's center of weight should be stable when moving; the bow step should be coordinated with the movements of brushing and pushing palms; the body is upright and feels comfortable; the movements are coordinated.

5. 进步搬拦捶 Jinbu banlanchui
(Stepping forward, Parrying, Blocking, and Punching)

（1）收脚握拳。（图6-59）

Move back your feet and clench your fist. (Fig. 6-59)

图 6-59　收脚握拳
Fig. 6-59 Move back your feet and clench your fist

（2）上步搬拳。（图6-60）

Step forward and parry the fist. (Fig. 6-60)

图 6-60　上步搬拳
Fig. 6-60 Step forward and parry the fist

（3）上步拦掌。（图6-61）

Step forward and block the palm. (Fig. 6-61)

图 6-61　上步拦掌

Fig. 6-61　Step forward and block the palm

（4）弓步冲拳。（图6-62）

Punch with a bow step. (Fig. 6-62)

图 6-62　弓步冲拳

Fig. 6-62　Punch with a bow step

要点：搬拳和拦掌有弧度，右拳向前冲打与弓步协调一致，舒展和顺，圆活完整。

Key points: Form an arc when parring the fist and blocking the palm; the right fist punches forward in harmony with the bow step; the movement is smooth, flexible and complete.

6. 如封似闭   Rufengsibi (Pushing one's Hands forward in Defence)

（1）翻掌回收。（图6-63）

Turn palms over and pull them back. (Fig. 6-63)

图 6-63　翻掌回收

Fig. 6-63 Turn palms over and pull them back

（2）弓步按推。（图6-64）

Push your palms with a bow step. (Fig. 6-64)

图 6-64　弓步按推

Fig. 6-64 Push your palms with a bow step

要点：身体后坐时，上体不可后仰或凸臀前俯；向前按推时，两手须走曲线，沿立圆进行，勿抬肘直臂。

Key points: When sitting back, don't lean back or protrude the hips or lean forward; when pushed forward, both hands should follow the curve and the vertical circle. Do not lift the elbow or straighten the arm.

7. 单鞭   Danbian (Single Whip)

（1）转身摆掌。（图6-65）

Turn around and swing your palms. (Fig. 6-65)

图 6-65　转身摆掌
Fig. 6-65 Turn around and swing your palms

（2）收脚勾手。（图6-66）

Move back the feet and hook the palms. (Fig. 6-66)

图 6-66　收脚勾手
Fig. 6-66 Move back the feet and hook the palms

（3）弓步推掌。（图6-67）

Push the palm forward with a bow step. (Fig. 6-67)

图 6-67　弓步推掌
Fig. 6-67 Push the palm forward with a bow step

要点：弓步时前腿膝关节垂直于脚面且不超过脚尖，后脚脚跟踏实；弓步与推掌协调一致。

Key points: When making a bow step, the knee joints of the front leg keep perpendicular to the instep and do not exceed the tiptoes; the heel of the rear leg is steady; the bow step is coordinated with the movement of palm pushing.

8. 手挥琵琶　　　　　　　　　Shouhuipipa (Hand Playing the Lute)

（1）跟步摆掌。（图6-68）

Step forward and swing your palms. (Fig. 6-68)

图 6-68　跟步摆掌
Fig. 6-68 Step forward and swing your palms

（2）虚步合掌。（图6-69）

Bring your palms together with an empty step. (Fig. 6-69)

图 6-69　虚步合掌

Fig. 6-69　Bring your palms together with an empty step

要点：完成虚步合掌动作时，两肩要松沉，两臂要有合劲；身体保持自然平稳。

Key points: When completing the movement of bringing palms' together with an empty step, relax and drop your shoulders; accumulate power on your arms; the body should be natural and stable.

第二段　The Second Section

9. 倒卷肱　　　　　　　　　Daojuanhong (Stepping back and Curling Arms)

（1）转体举掌。（图6–70）

Turn the body and raise the palms. (Fig. 6-70)

图 6–70　转体举掌
Fig. 6-70 Turn the body and raise the palms

（2）虚步推掌。（图6–71）

Push the palm with an empty step. (Fig. 6-71)

图 6–71　虚步推掌
Fig. 6-71 Push the palm with an empty step

（3）转体举掌。（图6-72）

Turn the body and raise the palms. (Fig. 6-72)

图 6-72　转体举掌
Fig. 6-72 Turn the body and raise the palms

（4）虚步推掌。（图6-73）

Push the palm with an empty step. (Fig. 6-73)

图 6-73　虚步推掌
Fig. 6-73 Push the palm with an empty step

要点：退步时，脚不可抬过高；移动时身体重心平稳，不可左右歪斜；虚步与推掌、顶肘协调配合。

Key points: Do not raise the feet too high when taking the feet back; when you move, the body's center of weight is stable, and make sure the body is not skewing; the empty step should be coordinated with palms and elbows.

10. 左右穿梭　　　　Zuoyou chuansuo (Moving the Shuttle on both Sides)

（1）收脚抱掌。（图6-74）

Move back your feet and make a ball-holding gesture. (Fig. 6-74)

图 6-74　收脚抱掌
Fig. 6-74　Move back your feet and make a ball-holding gesture

（2）弓步架推。（图6-75）

Block and push palms with a bow step. (Fig. 6-75)

图 6-75　弓步架推
Fig. 6-75　Block and push palms with a bow step

153

（3）收脚抱掌。（图6-76）

Move back your feet and make a ball-holding gesture. (Fig. 6-76)

图 6-76　收脚抱掌

Fig. 6-76　Move back your feet and make a ball-holding gestures

（4）弓步架推。（图6-77）

Block and push palms with a bow step. (Fig. 6-77)

图 6-77　弓步架推

Fig. 6-77　Block and push palms with a bow step

要点：上体不可前俯或左右倾斜，手向上举时要防止引肩上耸；一手上举，另一手前推要与弓腿协调一致。

Key points: The upper body should not bend forward or tilt left and right. When the hand is raised upward, it shall be prevented from leading the shoulder up; raise one hand and push the other forward in harmony with a bow step.

11. 海底针　　　　　　　　　Haidizhen (Needle at the Bottom of the Sea)

虚步插掌。（图6-78）

Thrust the palm with an empty step. (Fig. 6-78)

图 6-78　海底针
Fig. 6-78 Needle at the Bottom of the Sea

要点：上体不可太前倾，避免低头和臀部外凸；左腿膝关节要微屈，虚步插掌时上体要舒展伸拔。

Key points: The upper body should not lean forward too much, avoiding lowering the head and protruding buttocks; the left knee should be slightly bent, and the upper body should be stretched and pulled out when thrusting the palm with an empty step.

12. 闪通背　　　　　　　Shantongbei (Deflecting through the Arms)

弓步架推。（图6-79）

Block and push arms with a bow step. (Fig. 6-79)

图 6-79　闪通背
Fig. 6-79 Shantongbei (Deflecting through the arms)

要点： 上体自然正直，腰、胯松沉；推掌、举臂和弓腿动作协调一致。

Key points: The upper body is naturally straight; the waist and hips are relaxed and steady; the movements of palm pushing, arm raising and bowing are coordinated.

13. 云手　　　　　　　　　　Yunshou (Waving Hands like Clouds)

（1）弓步举掌。（图6-80）

Raise the palm with a bow step. (Fig. 6-80)

图 6-80　弓步举掌
Fig. 6-80 Raise the palm with a bow step

（2）收步云掌。（图6-81）

Step back and wave your palms. (Fig. 6-81)

图 6-81　收步云掌
Fig. 6-81　Step back and wave your palms

（3）开步云掌。（图6-82）

Wave your palms with an open step. (Fig. 6-82)

图 6-82　开步云掌
Fig. 6-82　Wave your palms with an open step

（4）收步云掌。（图6-83）

Step back and wave your palms. (Fig. 6-83)

图 6-83　收步云掌
Fig. 6-83 Step back and wave your palms

要点：以腰为轴，带动两手在体前翻、转、拧、裹、立圆、云拨，手高不过眉；下肢移动时，身体重心要稳定；眼的视线要随上手而移动，眼神与动作配合。

Key points: Taking the waist as the axis, drive the two hands to turn around, twist, draw,circle and wave in front of the body. Two hands are at the same height as eyebrows. When the lower limbs are moving, the body should be stable. Eyes move with the upper hand and are coordinated with movements.

14. 左右揽雀尾

（1）收脚抱掌。（图6-84）

Move back the feet and make a ball-holding gesture. (Fig. 6-84)

图 6-84 收脚抱掌

Fig. 6-84 Move back the feet and make a ball-holding gesture

（2）弓步前掤。（图6-85）

Ward off with a bow step. (Fig. 6-85)

图 6-85 弓步前掤

Fig. 6-85 Warding off with a bow step

（3）转体下捋。（图6-86）

Roll back and turn the body. (Fig. 6-86)

图 6-86　转体下捋

Fig. 6-86 Roll back and turn the body

（4）弓步前挤。（图6-87）

Press forward with a bow step. (Fig. 6-87)

图 6-87　弓步前挤

Fig. 6-87 Press forward with a bow step

（5）后坐下按。（图6-88）

Sit back and press down palms. (Fig. 6-88)

图 6-88　后坐下按
Fig. 6-88 Sit back and press down palms

（6）弓步按推。（图6-89）

Push your palms forward with a bow step. (Fig. 6-89)

图 6-89　弓步按推
Fig. 6-89 Push your palms forward with a bow step

（7）收脚抱掌。（图6-90）

Move back the feet and make a ball-holding gesture. (Fig. 6-90)

图 6-90　收脚抱掌

Fig. 6-90　Move back the feet and make a ball-holding gesture

（8）弓步前掤。（图6-91）

Ward off with a bow step. (Fig. 6-91)

图 6-91　弓步前掤

Fig. 6-91　Ward off with a bow step

（9）转体下捋。（图6−92）

Roll back and turn the body. (Fig. 6-92)

图 6−92　转体下捋
Fig. 6-92 Roll back and turn the body

（10）弓步前挤。（图6−93）

Press forward with a bow step. (Fig. 6-93)

图 6−93　弓步前挤
Fig. 6-93 Press forward with a bow step

（11）后坐下按。（图6-94）

Sit back and press down palms. (Fig. 6-94)

图 6-94　后坐下按
Fig. 6-94 Sit back and press down palms

（12）弓步按推。（图6-95）

Push your palms forward with a bow step. (Fig. 6-95)

图 6-95　弓步按推
Fig. 6-95 Push your palms forward with a bow step

要点：弓步掤臂呈弧形，腕与肩平；两手下捋沿弧线运行，下捋时重心后移，两腿虚实分明，上体保持中正；弓步前挤时两臂向前撑圆；两掌按推，两臂沿立圆运行；弓步与掤臂、前挤、按推协调配合。

Key points: In a bow step, ward off arms in a curve and maintain wrists and shoulders at the same height; the hands move along the arc when pressed down, and the body's center of weight moves backward; make a clear distincion between emptiness and solidness on the legs, and the upper body remains erect; press forward in a bow step and stretch two arms; push two palms forward, and two arms run along the circle; the bow step is coordinated the movements of warding-off, pushing and pressing arms.

15. 十字手   Shizishou (Cross Arms)

（1）弓步摆掌。（图6-96）

Swing your palms with a bow step. (Fig. 6-96)

图 6-96　弓步摆掌

Fig. 6-96 Swing your palms with a bow step

（2）开立抱掌。（图6-97）

Cross arms with an open step. (Fig. 6-97)

图 6-97　开立抱掌

Fig. 6-97 Cross arms with an open step

要点：平行步时两掌交叉十字合抱于体前，两臂保持弧形，圆满舒适，沉肩坠肘。

Key points: Cross your arms in front of the body in a parallel step, keep your arms in an arc shape, round and comfortable; sink your shoulders and drop your elbows.

16. 收势　　　　　　　　　　　　　　　　　Closing Posture

（1）翻掌分手。（图6-98）

Turn your palms over and separate your hands. (Fig. 6-98)

图 6-98　翻掌分手

Fig. 6-98 Turn your palms over and separate your hands

（2）垂臂按掌。（图6-99）

Drop your arms and press down your palms. (Fig. 6-99)

图 6-99　垂臂按掌

Fig. 6-99 Drop your arms and press down your palms

（3）收脚并步。（图6-100）

Take your feet back and stand with your feet together. (Fig. 6-100)

图 6-100　收脚并步

Fig. 6-100 Take your feet back and stand with your feet together

要点：中正圆活，轻灵沉稳，平和自然，无过不及。

Key points: The movement is smooth and lively, light and steady, peaceful and natural without excess and deficiency.

练习二段太极拳结束后行抱拳礼。

At the end of your practice, perform the palm-fist salute.

三段太极拳 Taijiquan: Grade 3

动作名称

预备势

第一段

1. 起势
2. 左右野马分鬃
3. 白鹤亮翅
4. 左右搂膝拗步
5. 手挥琵琶

第二段

6. 左右倒卷肱
7. 左揽雀尾
8. 右揽雀尾
9. 单鞭

第三段

10. 云手
11. 单鞭

12. 高探马
13. 右蹬脚
14. 双峰贯耳
15. 转身左蹬脚

第四段

16. 左下势独立
17. 右下势独立
18. 左右穿梭
19. 海底针
20. 闪通背
21. 转身搬拦捶
22. 如封似闭
23. 十字手
24. 收势

三段太极拳
Taijiquan: Grade 3

Names of Actions

Preparatory Posture

The First Section

1. Commencing Posture

2. Zuoyou Yemafenzong (Parting the Wild Horse's Mane on both Sides)

3. Baiheliangchi (White Crane Spreading Its Wings)

4. Zuoyou Louxi'aobu (Brushing Knees and Twisting Steps on both Sides)

5. Shouhuipipa (Hand Playing the Lute)

The Second Section

6. Zuoyou Daojuanhong (Stepping back and Curling Arms on both Sides)

7. Zuo Lanquewei (Grasping the Peacock's Tail on Left Side)

8. You Lanquewei (Grasping the Peacock's Tail on Right Side)

9. Danbian (Single Whip)

The Third Section

10. Yunshou (Waving Hands like Clouds)

11. Danbian (Single Whip)

12. Gaotanma (Patting the High Horse)

13. Right Heel Kick

14. Shuangfengguaner (Striking the Opponent's Ears with both Fists)

15. Turning and Kicking with Left Heel

The Forth Section

16. Snake Creeping Down, Left Side

17. Snake Creeping Down, Right Side

18. Zuoyou Chuansuo (Moving the Shuttle on both Sides)

19. Haidizhen (Needle at the Bottom of the Sea)

20. Shantongbei (Deflecting through the Arms)

21. Zhuanshen Banlanchui (Turning Body, Parrying, Blocking and Punching)

22. Rufengsibi (Pushing one's Hands forward in Defence)

23. Shizishou (Cross Arms)

24. Closing Posture

练习三段太极拳开始前行抱拳礼。

Before your practice, perform the palm-fist salute.

预备势   Preparatory Posture

并步站立。（图6-101）

Stand with your feet together. (Fig. 6-101)

图 6-101　并步站立

Fig. 6-101 Stand with your feet together

要点：口闭齿扣，舌抵上腭；上悬下沉，中节舒松；精神集中，心平气和，呼吸自然。

Key points: The mouth is closed, and the tongue is pressed against the palate; the head is pulled up and the lower pant is stable with the middle section relaxed; be concentrated and calm with natural breath.

第一段 The First Section

1.起势   Commencing Posture

（1）开步站立。（图6-102）

Stand with your feet apart. (Fig. 6-102)

图 6-102　开步直立
Fig. 6-102 Stand with your feet apart

（2）两臂前举。（图6-103）

Raise your arms forward. (Fig. 6-103)

图 6-103　两臂前举
Fig. 6-103 Raise your arms forward

（3）屈膝按掌。（图6-104）

Bend knees and press palms down. (Fig. 6-104)

图 6-104　屈膝按掌

Fig. 6-104 Bend knees and press palms down

要点：身型要求松胯敛臀，含胸拔背，沉肩坠肘，虚领顶劲；下按掌掌指舒展，掌心微含；中正安舒，气沉丹田，松静自然。

Key points: Relax the crotch and clench the buttock, relax the chest and draw the back, sink the shoulders and drop the elbows, and pull up the head and relax the neck; press the palms down, stretch the palms and fingers, and the palms slightly shape a circle and maintain it; keep the body upright, calm and comfortable; gather Qi into Dantian and be relaxed, quiet and natural.

2. 左右野马分鬃　　　　　　　　　　　　　Zuoyou Yemafenzong
(Parting the Wild Horse's Mane on both Sides)

（1）收脚抱掌。（图6-105）

Move back your feet and make a ball-holding gesture. (Fig. 6-105)

图 6-105　收脚抱掌
Fig. 6-105　Move back your feet and make a ball-holding gesture

（2）弓步分掌。（图6-106）

Separate palms with a bow step. (Fig. 6-106)

图 6-106　弓步分掌
Fig. 6-106　Separate palms with a bow step

（3）收脚抱掌。（图6-107）

Move back your feet and make a ball-holding gesture. (Fig. 6-107)

图 6-107　收脚抱掌

Fig. 6-107　Move back your feet and make a ball-holding gesture

（4）弓步分掌。（图6-108）

Separate palms with a bow step. (Fig. 6-108)

图 6-108　弓步分掌

Fig. 6-108　Separate palms with a bow step

（5）收脚抱掌。（图6-109）

Move back your feet and make a ball-holding gesture. (Fig. 6-109)

图 6-109　收脚抱掌
Fig. 6-109 Move back your feet and make a ball-holding gesture

（6）弓步分掌。（图6-110）

Separate palms with a bow step. (Fig. 6-110)

图 6-110　弓步分掌
Fig. 6-110 Separate palms with a bow step

要点： 弓步斜分掌时两臂保持弧形，弓步与分掌协调配合；身体重心转换保持平稳，势正招圆。

Key points: When separating palms with a bow step, the arms should be arc-shaped, and the bow step and the separation should be coordinated; the shift of the body's center of weight should be kept stable, and the body should be upright and the movements should be smooth and flexible.

3.白鹤亮翅　　　　　　　Baiheliangchi (White Crane Spreading Its Wings)

（1）跟步抱掌。（图6-111）

Make a ball-holding gesture when moving one leg forward. (Fig. 6-111)

图 6-111　跟步抱掌

Fig. 6-111 Make a ball-holding gesture when moving one leg forward

（2）虚步挑掌。（图6-112）

Lift the palms in an empty step. (Fig. 6-112)

图 6-112　虚步挑掌

Fig. 6-112 Lift the palms in an empty step

要点：虚步时后脚脚跟踏实。虚步与挑掌、按掌协调配合，上下相随，虚实分明。

Key points: The heel is stable when making an empty step. the empty step is coordinated with the movements of palm lifting and palm pressing, the upper and lower parts of the body should be coordinated and make a clear distinction between emptiness and solidness.

4.左右搂膝拗步   Zuoyou Louxi'aobu
(Brushing Knees and Twisting Steps on both Sides)

（1）收脚举掌。（图6-113）

Move your feet back and raise your palms. (Fig. 6-113)

图 6-113　收脚举掌

Fig. 6-113　Move your feet back and raise your palms

（2）弓步搂推。（图6-114）

Brush aside and push the palm with a bow step. (Fig. 6-114)

图 6-114　弓步搂推

Fig. 6-114 Brush aside and push the palm with a bow step

（3）收脚举掌。（图6-115）

Move your feet back and raise your palms. (Fig. 6-115)

图 6-115　收脚举掌
Fig. 6-115 Move your feet back and raise your palms

（4）弓步搂推。（图6-116）

Brush aside and push the palm with a bow step. (Fig. 6-116)

图 6-116　弓步搂推
Fig. 6-116 Brush aside and push the palm with bow step

（5）收脚举掌。（图6-117）

Move your feet back and raise your palms. (Fig. 6-117)

图 6-117　收脚举掌

Fig. 6-117 Move your feet back and raise your palms

（6）弓步搂推。（图6-118）

Brush aside and push the palm with a bow step. (Fig. 6-118)

图 6-118　弓步搂推

Fig. 6-118 Brush aside and push the palm with a bow step

要点： 上步时后脚不可拖地，移动时身体重心平稳，弓步与搂掌、推掌协调配合；中正安舒，动静有序。

Key points: When stepping forward, the heels should not be dragged and raised too high; the body's center of weight should be stable when moving; the bow step should be coordinated with the movements of palm brushing and pushing; the body is upright and feels comfortable; the movements are coordinated.

5.手挥琵琶   Shouhuipipa (Hand Playing the Lute)

（1）跟步伸掌。（图6-119）

Step forward and stretch your palms. (Fig. 6-119)

图 6-119 跟步伸掌
Fig. 6-119 Step forward and stretch your palms

（2）后坐转体。（图6-120）

Sit back and turn around. (Fig. 6-120)

图 6-120 后坐转体
Fig. 6-120 Sit back and turn around

（3）虚步合掌。（图6-121）

Bring your palms together with an empty step. (Fig. 6-121)

图 6-121　虚步合掌
Fig. 6-121 Bring your palms together with an empty step

要点：身体重心后移和左手上起、右手回收要协调一致；以腰为轴，带动四肢，身法与手法要协调配合，屈膝、松胯、敛臀。

Key points: Coordinate the retraction of the body's center of weight with the lifting of the left hand and the retraction of the right hand. Take the waist as the axis to drive the limbs, and coordinate the body with hand movements. Bend the knees, relax the crotch, and clench the buttocks.

第二段 The Second Section

6. 左右倒卷肱
Zuoyou Daojuanhong
(Stepping back and Curling Arms on both Sides)

（1）转体举掌。（图6-122）

Turn the body and raise palms. (Fig. 6-122)

图 6-122　转体举掌
Fig. 6-122 Turn the body and raise palms

（2）虚步推掌。（图6-123）

Push the palm with an empty step. (Fig. 6-123)

图 6-123　虚步推掌
Fig. 6-123 Push the palm with an empty step

（3）转体举掌。（图6-124）

Turn the body and raise palms. (Fig. 6-124)

图 6-124　转体举掌
Fig. 6-124 Turn the body and raise palms

（4）虚步推掌。（图6-125）

Push the palm with an empty step. (Fig. 6-125)

图 6-125　虚步推掌
Fig. 6-125 Push the palm with an empty step

（5）转体举掌。（图6-126）

Turn the body and raise palms. (Fig. 6-126)

图 6-126　转体举掌

Fig. 6-126 Turn the body and raise palms

（6）虚步推掌。（图6-127）

Push the palm with an empty step. (Fig. 6-127)

图 6-127　虚步推掌

Fig. 6-127 Push the palm with an empty step

（7）转体举掌。（图6-128）

Turn the body and raise palms. (Fig. 6-128)

图 6-128　转体举掌
Fig. 6-128 Turn the body and raise palms

（8）虚步推掌。（图6-129）

Push the palm with an empty step. (Fig. 6-129)

图 6-129　虚步推掌
Fig. 6-129 Push the palm with an empty step

要点： 移动时身体重心平稳，不可左右歪斜；虚步与推掌、顶肘协调配合。

Key points: When moving, the body's center of weight is stable, and make sure the body is not skewing; the empty step should be coordinated with palms and elbows.

7. 左揽雀尾　　　Zuo Lanquewei (Grasping the Peacock's Tail on Left Side)

（1）收脚抱掌。（图6-130）

Move back your feet and make a ball-holding gesture. (Fig. 6-130)

图 6-130　收脚抱掌

Fig. 6-130　Move back your feet and make a ball-holding gesture

（2）弓步前掤。（图6-131）

Ward off with a bow step. (Fig. 6-131)

图 6-131　弓步前掤

Fig. 6-131 Ward off with a bow step

（3）转体下捋。（图6-132）

Roll back and turn the body. (Fig. 6-132)

图 6-132　转体下捋
Fig. 6-132 Roll back and turn the body

（4）弓步前挤。（图6-133）

Press forward with a bow step. (Fig. 6-133)

图 6-133　弓步前挤
Fig. 6-133 Press forward with a bow step

（5）后坐下按。（图6-134）

Sit back and press down palms. (Fig. 6-134)

图 6-134　后坐下按
Fig. 6-134 Sit back and press down palms

（6）弓步按推。（图6-135）

Push your palms forward with a bow step. (Fig. 6-135)

图 6-135　弓步按推
Fig. 6-135 Push your palms forward with a bow step

要点：弓步掤臂呈弧形，腕与肩平；两手下捋沿弧线运行，下捋时重心后移，两腿虚实分明，上体保持中正；弓步前挤时两臂向前撑圆；两掌按推，两臂沿立圆运行；弓步与掤臂、前挤、按推协调配合。

Key points: In a bow step, ward off arms in a curve and maintain wrists and shoulders at the same height; the hands move along the arc when pressed down, and the body's center of weight moves backward; make a clear distincion between emptiness and solidness on the legs, and the upper body remains erect; press forward in a bow step and stretch two arms; push two palms forward, and two arms run along the circle; the bow step is coordinated the movements of warding-off, pushing and pressing arms.

8.右揽雀尾　　　　You Lanquewei(Grasping the Peacock's Tail on Right Side)

（1）收脚抱掌。（图6-136）

Move back your feet and make a ball-holding gesture. (Fig. 6-136)

图 6-136　收脚抱掌

Fig. 6-136 Move back your feet and make a ball-holding gesture

（2）弓步前掤。（图6-137）

Ward off with a bow step. (Fig. 6-137)

图 6-137　弓步前掤
Fig. 6-137 Ward off with a bow step

（3）转体下捋。（图6-138）

Roll back and turn the body. (Fig. 6-138)

图 6-138　转体下捋
Fig. 6-138 Roll back and turn the body

（4）弓步前挤。（图6-139）

Press forward with a bow step. (Fig. 6-139)

图 6-139　弓步前挤
Fig. 6-139　Press forward with a bow step

（5）后坐下按。（图6-140）

Sit back and press down palms. (Fig. 6-140)

图 6-140　后坐下按
Fig. 6-140　Sit back and press down palms

（6）弓步按推。（图6-141）

Push your palms forward with a bow step. (Fig. 6-141)

图 6-141　弓步按推

Fig. 6-141 Push your palms forward with a bow step

要点： 弓步掤臂呈弧形，腕与肩平；两手下捋沿弧线运行，下捋时重心后移，两腿虚实分明，上体保持中正；弓步前挤时两臂向前撑圆；两掌按推，两臂沿立圆运行；弓步与掤臂、前挤、按推协调配合。

Key points: In a bow step, ward off arms in a curve and maintain wrists and shoulders at the same height; the hands move along the arc when pressed down, and the body's center of weight moves backward; make a clear distincion between emptiness and solidness on the legs, and the upper body remains erect; press forward in a bow step and stretch two arms; push two palms forward, and two arms run along the circle; the bow step is coordinated the movements of warding-off, pushing and pressing arms.

（1）碾步摆掌。（图6-142）

Grind your steps and swing your palms. (Fig. 6-142)

图 6-142　碾步摆掌
Fig. 6-142 Grind your steps and swing your palms

（2）收脚勾手。（图6-143）

Move back the feet and hook the hand. (Fig. 6-143)

图 6-143　收脚勾手
Fig. 6-143 Move back the feet and hook the hand

（3）转体上步。（图6-144）

Turn the body and step forward. (Fig. 6-144)

图 6-144　转体上步
Fig. 6-144 Turn the body and step forward

（4）弓步推掌。（图6-145）

Push the palm with a bow step. (Fig. 6-145)

图 6-145　弓步推掌
Fig. 6-145 Push the palm with a bow step

要点：弓步时前腿膝关节垂直于脚面且不超过脚尖，后脚脚跟踏实；弓步与推掌协调一致。

Key points: When making the bow step, the knee joint of the front leg keeps perpendicular to the instep and does not exceed the tiptoes, and the heel of the rear leg is steady; the bow step is coordinated with the movement of palm pushing.

第三段　The Third Section

10. 云手　　　　　　　　　Yunshou (Waving Hands like Clouds)

（1）碾步摆掌。（图6–146）

Grind your steps and swing your palms. (Fig. 6-146)

图 6–146　碾步摆掌

Fig. 6-146　Grind your steps and swing your palms

（2）收步云掌。（图6–147）

Step back and wave your palms. (Fig. 6-147)

图 6–147　收步云掌

Fig. 6-147　Step back and wave your palms

（3）开步云掌。（图6-148）

Wave your palms with an open step. (Fig. 6-148)

图 6-148　开步云掌

Fig. 6-148 Wave your palms with an open step

（4）收步云掌。（图6-149）

Step back and wave your palms. (Fig. 6-149)

图 6-149　收步云掌

Fig. 6-149 Step back and wave your palms

（5）开步云掌。（图6-150）

Wave your palms with an open step. (Fig. 6-150)

图 6-150　开步云掌
Fig. 6-150 Wave your palms with an open step

（6）收步云掌。（图6-151）

Step back and wave your palms. (Fig. 6-151)

图 6-151　收步云掌
Fig. 6-151 Step back and wave your palms

要点：身体转动要以腰为轴，带动两手在体前翻、转、拧、裹、立圆、云拨，手高不过眉；下肢移动时，身体重心要稳定；眼的视线要随上手移动，眼神与动作要协调配合。

Key points: Taking the waist as the axis, drive the two hands to turn around, twist, draw,circle and wave in front of the body. Two hands are at the same height as eyebrows. When the lower limbs are moving, the body should be stable. Eyes move with the upper hand and are coordinated with movements.

11. 单鞭 Danbian (Single Whip)

（1）收脚勾手。（图6-152）

Move back the feet and hook the hand. (Fig. 6-152)

图 6-152　收脚勾手
Fig. 6-152 Move back the feet and hook the hand

（2）转体上步。（图6-153）

Turn the body and step forward. (Fig. 6-153)

图 6-153　转体上步
Fig. 6-153 Turn the body and step forward

（3）弓步推掌。（图6-154）

Push the palm forward with a bow step. (Fig. 6-154)

图 6-154　弓步推掌

Fig. 6-154 Push the palm forward with a bow step

要点：弓步时前腿膝关节垂直于脚背面不超过脚尖，后脚脚跟踏实；弓步与推掌协调一致。

Key points: When making a bow step, the knee joint of the front leg keeps perpendicular to the instep and does not exceed the tiptoes; the heel of the rear leg is steady; the bow step is coordinated with the movement palm pushing.

12. 高探马　　　　　　　　　　Gaotanma (Patting the High Horse)

（1）跟步翻掌。（图6-155）

Step forward and flip palms. (Fig. 6-155)

图 6-155　跟步翻掌

Fig. 6-155 Step forward and flip palms

（2）虚步推掌。（图6-156）

Push your palms with an empty step. (Fig. 6-156)

图 6-156　虚步推掌

Fig. 6-156 Push your palms with an empty step

要点： 跟步移动转换身体重心时，身体不要有起伏；虚步推掌应在转腰顺肩的配合下完成，身体保持中正、舒展，动作协调一致。

Key points: When you step forward to change the center of weight, the body should not fluctuate; the palm-pushing gesture with an empty step should be completed with the cooperation of turning the waist along the shoulder; keep the body upright and stretched, and the movements are coordinated.

13. 右蹬脚　　　　　　　　　　　　　　　　Right Heel Kick

（1）提脚穿掌。（图6-157）

Lift the foot and thrust the palm. (Fig. 6-157)

图 6-157　提脚穿掌

Fig. 6-157 Lift the foot and thrust the palm

（2）上步翻掌。（图6-158）

Step forward and flip your palms. (Fig. 6-158)

图 6-158　上步翻掌
Fig. 6-158 Step forward and flip your palms

（3）弓腿分掌。（图6-159）

Separate palms with a bow step. (Fig. 6-159)

图 6-159　弓腿分掌
Fig. 6-159 Separate palms with a bow step

（4）提膝抱掌。（图6-160）

Lift the knee and make a ball-holding gesture. (Fig. 6-160)

图 6-160　提膝抱掌

Fig. 6-160　Lift the knee and make a ball-holding gesture

（5）蹬脚分掌。（图6-161）

Kick and separate your palms. (Fig. 6-161)

图 6-161　蹬脚分掌

Fig. 6-161　Kick and separate your palms

要点：右臂和右腿上下相对，身体要稳定，不可前俯后仰；上举腿要伸直，蹬脚不低于水平位；分掌与蹬脚协调一致。

Key points: The right arm and the right leg are in the same sagittal level; the body should be stable, and not bend forward or backward; the upper leg should be straightened, and the position of kicking foot should not be lower than the horizontal level; the movements of seperating palms and kicking heels should be coordinated.

14. 双峰贯耳　Shuangfengguaner (Striking the Opponent's Ears with both Fists)

（1）屈膝落掌。（图6-162）

Bend your knees and drop your palms. (Fig. 6-162)

图 6-162　屈膝落掌

Fig. 6-162　Bend your knees and drop your palms

（2）落步收拳。（图6-163）

Step down and take your fists back. (Fig. 6-163)

图 6-163　落步收拳

Fig. 6-163　Step down and take your fists back

（3）弓步贯拳。（图6-164）

Sweep side punch with a bow step. (Fig. 6-164)

图 6-164　弓步贯拳

Fig. 6-164 Sweep side punch with a bow step

要点：沉肩坠肘，两臂均保持弧形；重心前移成弓步与两掌变拳自下经两侧向前上方弧形圈打协调配合，沉稳浑厚，棉里藏针。

Key points: Sink the shoulders and drop the elbows, and keep both arms in an arc. The center of weight moves forward into a bow step and the two palms change into fists from the bottom to the top in a curve through both sides. The movement is stable and the strength is held in softness.

15. 转身左蹬脚   Turning and Kicking with Left Heel

（1）蹍步分掌。（图6-165）

Grind steps and separate palms. (Fig. 6-165)

图 6-165　蹍步分掌

Fig. 6-165 Grind steps and separate palms

（2）提膝抱掌。（图6-166）

Lift the knee and make a ball-holding gesture. (Fig. 6-166)

图 6-166　提膝抱掌
Fig. 6-166 Lift the knee and make a ball-holding gesture

（3）蹬脚分掌。（图6-167）

Kick with a heel and separate palms. (Fig. 6-167)

图 6-167　蹬脚分掌
Fig. 6-167 Kick with a heel and separate palms

要点：左臂和左腿上下相对，身体要稳定，不可前俯后仰，上举腿要伸直，蹬脚不低于水平位；蹬脚与分掌协调一致；转接柔顺，不偏不倚。

Key points: The left arm and the left leg are facing each other; the body must be stable and not bend forward or backward; the upper leg must be straight, and the position of heel kicking should not be lower than the horizontal level; the movements of separating palms and kicking heels should be coordinated. The transition is smooth without skewing.

第四段　The Forth Section

16. 左下势独立　　　　　　　　　Snake Creeping down, Left Side

（1）收腿勾手。（图6-168）

Move the leg back and hook hands. (Fig. 6-168)

图 6-168　收腿勾手
Fig. 6-168 Move the leg back and hook hands

（2）屈蹲开步。（图6-169）

Bend the knee to make a bow step. (Fig. 6-169)

图 6-169　屈蹲开步
Fig. 6-169 Bend the knee to make a bow step

（3）仆步穿掌。（图6-170）

Thrust the palm with a crouching step. (Fig. 6-170)

图 6-170　仆步穿掌
Fig. 6-170 Thrust the palm with a crouching step

（4）弓步挑掌。（图6-171）

Lift the palm with a bow step. (Fig. 6-171)

图 6-171　弓步挑掌
Fig. 6-171 Lift the palm with a bow step

（5）独立挑掌。（图6-172）

Lift the palm and stand on one leg. (Fig. 6-172)

图 6-172　独立挑掌
Fig. 6-172 Lift the palm and stand on one leg

要点：仆步穿掌时，上体不要前俯；仆步时屈蹲腿全蹲，平铺腿伸直，全脚掌内扣着地；提膝与挑掌协调一致，同时，按掌在胯旁；上提腿大腿勿低于水平位。

Key points: When thrusting the palm with a crouching step, don't lean forward; when making a crouching step, bend the squatting legs, squat fully, straighten the tiled legs, and buckle the whole soles of the feet to the ground. Lift the knee and snap the palm simultaneously. At the same time, press the palm close to the crotch; lift the leg and maintain the position of the thighs not lower than the horizontal level.

17. 右下势独立   Snake Creeping down, Right Side

（1）落步勾手。（图6-173）

Step down and hook hands. (Fig. 6-173)

图 6-173　落步勾手
Fig. 6-173 Step down and hook hands

（2）屈蹲开步。（图6-174）

Bend the knee to make a bow step. (Fig. 6-174)

图 6-174　屈蹲开步
Fig. 6-174 Bend the knee to make a bow step

（3）仆步穿掌。（图6-175）

Thrust the palm with a crouching step. (Fig. 6-175)

图 6-175　仆步穿掌

Fig. 6-175 Thrust the palm with a crouching step

（4）弓步挑掌。（图6-176）

Lift the palm with a bow step. (Fig. 6-176)

图 6-176　弓步挑掌

Fig. 6-176 Lift the palm with a bow step

（5）独立挑掌。（图6-177）

Lift the palm and stand on one leg. (Fig. 6-177)

图 6-177　独立挑掌

Fig. 6-177 Lift the palm and stand on one leg

要点：仆步穿掌时，上体不要前俯；仆步时屈蹲腿全蹲，平铺腿伸直，全脚掌内扣着地；提膝与挑掌协调一致，同时，按掌在胯旁；上提腿大腿勿低于水平位。

Key points: When thrusting the palm with a crouching step, don't lean forward; when making a crouching step, bend the squatting legs, squat fully, straighten the tiled legs, and buckle the whole soles of the feet to the ground. Lift the knee and snap the palm simultaneously. At the same time, press the palm close to the crotch; lift the leg and maintain the position of the thighs not lower than the horizontal level.

18. 左右穿梭　　Zuoyou Chuansuo (Moving the Shuttle on both Sides)

（1）收脚抱掌。（图6-178）

Move back your feet and make a ball-holding gesture. (Fig. 6-178)

图 6-178　收脚抱掌
Fig. 6-178 Move back your feet and make a ball-holding gesture

（2）上步分掌。（图6-179）

Step forward and separate palms. (Fig. 6-179)

图 6-179　上步分掌
Fig. 6-179　Step forward and separate palms

（3）弓步架推。（图6-180）

Block and push palms with a bow step. (Fig. 6-180)

图 6-180　弓步架推
Fig. 6-180 Block and push palms with a bow step

（4）收脚抱掌。（图6-181）

Move back your feet and make a ball-holding gesture. (Fig. 6-181)

图 6-181　收脚抱掌
Fig. 6-181 Move back your feet and make a ball-holding gesture

（5）上步分掌。（图6-182）

Step forward and separate palms. (Fig. 6-182)

图 6-182　上步分掌
Fig. 6-182 Step forward and separate palms

（6）弓步架推。（图6-183）

Block and push palms with a bow step. (Fig. 6-183)

图 6-183　弓步架推
Fig. 6-183　Block and push palms with a bow step

要点：上体不可前俯或左右倾斜，手向上举时要防止引肩上耸；一手上举，另一手前推要与弓腿协调一致。

Key points: The upper body should not bend forward or tilt left and right. When the hands are raised upward, they shall be prevented from leading the shoulders up; raise one hand and push the other forward in harmony with the bow step.

19. 海底针   Haidizhen (Needle at the Bottom of the Sea)

（1）跟步提手。（图6-184）

Step forward and lift hands. (Fig. 6-184)

图 6-184 　跟步提手
Fig. 6-184 Step forward and lift hands

（2）虚步插掌。（图6-185）

Thrust the palm with an empty step. (Fig. 6-185)

图 6-185 　虚步插掌
Fig. 6-185 Thrust the palm with an empty step

要点： 上体不可太前倾，避免低头和臀部外凸；左腿膝关节要微屈，虚步插掌时上体要舒展伸拔。

Key points: The upper body should not lean forward too much, avoiding lowering the head and protruding buttocks; the left knee should be slightly bent, and the upper body should be stretched and pulled out when thrusting the palm in an empty step.

20. 闪通背 Shantongbei (Deflecting through the Arms)

（1）收脚提手。（图6-186）

Move back the feet and lift the hand. (Fig. 6-186)

图 6-186　收脚提手
Fig. 6-186 Move back the feet and lift the hand

（2）弓步架推。（图6-187）

Block and push arms with a bow step. (Fig. 6-187)

图 6-187　弓步架推
Fig. 6-187 Block and push arms with a bow step

要点：上体自然正直，腰、胯松沉；推掌、举臂和弓腿动作协调一致。

Key points: The upper body is naturally straight; the waist and hips are relaxed and steady; the movements of palm pushing, arm raising and bowing are coordinated.

21. 转身搬拦捶   Zhuanshen Banlanchui (Turning Body, Parrying, Blocking and Punching)

（1）碾步转体。（图6-188）

Grind steps and turn the body. (Fig. 6-188)

图 6-188　碾步转体

Fig. 6-188 Grind steps and turn the body

（2）坐腿握拳。（图6-189）

Sit on one leg and clench fists. (Fig. 6-189)

图 6-189　坐腿握拳

Fig. 6-189 Sit on one leg and clench fists

（3）摆步搬拳。（图6-190）

Step forward and parry the fist. (Fig. 6-190)

图 6-190　摆步搬拳
Fig. 6-190 Step forward and parry the fist

（4）转体摆掌。（图6-191）

Turn around and swing palms. (Fig. 6-191)

图 6-191　转体摆掌
Fig. 6-191 Turn around and swing palms

（5）上步拦掌。（图6-192）

Step forward and block the palm. (Fig. 6-192)

图 6-192　上步拦掌
Fig. 6-192 Step forward and block the palm

（6）弓步冲拳。（图6-193）

Punch with a bow step. (Fig. 6-193)

图 6-193　弓步冲拳
Fig 6-193 Punch with a bow step

要点： 搬拳和拦掌有弧度，右拳向前冲打与弓步协调一致，舒展和顺，圆活完整。

Key points: Form an arc when parring the fist and blocking the palm; the right fist punches forward in harmony with the bow step, stretching smoothly; the movement is flexible and complete.

22. 如封似闭   Rufengsibi (Pushing one's Hands forward in Defence)

（1）穿手变掌。（图6-194）

Thrust hands and change them into palms. (Fig. 6-194)

图 6-194　穿手变掌

Fig. 6-194 Thrust hands and change them into palms

（2）后坐收掌。（图6-195）

Sit back and retract palms. (Fig. 6-195)

图 6-195　后坐收掌

Fig. 6-195 Sit back and retract palms

（3）翻掌下按。（图6-196）

Flip palms and press them down. (Fig. 6-196)

图 6-196　翻掌下按
Fig. 6-196 Flip palms and press them down

（4）弓步按推。（图6-197）

Push palms with a bow step. (Fig. 6-197)

图 6-197　弓步按推
Fig. 6-197 Push palms with a bow step

要点：身体后坐时，上体不可后仰或凸臀前俯；向前按推时，两手须走曲线，沿立圆运行，勿抬肘直臂。

Key points: When sitting back, don't lean back or protrude the hips or lean forward; when pushed forward, both hands should follow the curve and the vertical circle. Do not lift elbows or straighten arms.

23. 十字手   Shizishou (Cross Arms)

（1）弓步摆掌。（图6-198）

Swing palms with a bow step. (Fig. 6-198)

图 6-198 弓步摆掌
Fig. 6-198 Swing palms with a bow step

（2）开立抱掌。（图6-199）

Make a ball-holding gesture with an open step. (Fig. 6-199)

图 6-199 开立抱掌
Fig. 6-199 Make a ball-holding gesture with an open step

要点：平行步时两掌交叉十字合抱于体前，两臂保持弧形，圆满舒适，沉肩坠肘。

Key points: Cross your arms in front of your body in a parallel step; keep your arms in an arc shape, round and comfortable; sink your shoulders and drop your elbows.

24. 收势 Closing Posture

（1）翻掌分手。（图6-200）

Turn palms over and separate hands. (Fig. 6-200)

图 6-200　翻掌分手
Fig. 6-200 Turn palms over and separate hands

（2）垂臂按掌。（图6-201）

Drop arms and press palms down. (Fig. 6-201)

图 6-201　垂臂按掌
Fig. 6-201 Drop arms and press palms down

（3）收脚并步。（图6-202）

Take your feet back and stand with your feet together. (Fig. 6-202)

图 6-202　收脚并步

Fig. 6-202 Take your feet back and stand with your feet together

要点：中正圆活，轻灵沉稳，平和自然，无过不及。

Key points: The movement is smooth and lively, light and steady, peaceful and natural without excess and deficiency.

练习三段太极拳结束后行抱拳礼。

At the end of your practice, perform the palm-fist salute.